RISE
of the
DEO

LEADERSHIP BY DESIGN

Maria Giudice   *Christopher Ireland*

New
Riders

VOICES THAT MATTER™

Rise of the DEO: Leadership by Design
Maria Giudice and Christopher Ireland

New Riders
www.newriders.com

To report errors, please send a note to errata@peachpit.com

New Riders is an imprint of Peachpit, a division of Pearson Education.

Copyright © 2014 by Maria Giudice and Christopher Ireland

ISBN 13:   978-0-321-93439-0
ISBN 10:   0-321-93439-3

9 8 7 6 5 4 3 2 1

Printed and bound in the United States of America

DEDICATION

*To Max, Olivia and Lilah —
our own future DEOs.*

*We can't wait to see the world
you will create.*

TABLE OF CONTENTS

DO

BE

NEXT

CHANGE

The crowd at SXSW stretches to the horizon. The two-week-long conference showcasing music, film, and interactive talent attracts a young crowd. Mostly under 40, the attendees come from around the globe for a hit of their favorite drug: change.

Change used to be much less popular. In business, it was an outcome: the result of deliberate, often measured efforts to reach a new goal or solve a significant problem. Considered inherently risky, it was administered in small doses. We welcomed a refreshed logo or name. A minor feature could be advertised as "new and improved," but large-scale change signaled distress. Big change meant something was wrong. Big change meant someone had erred. Today, while change retains its prescriptive quality in some circumstances, for most businesses, and certainly for the 60,000 paid attendees at SXSW, it's in the bloodstream.

No organization is static right now. Even the most staid and conservative company changes simply by staying the same while everything around it evolves. Traditional companies become dated companies through no effort of their own. They become the 1950s suburban ranch home surrounded on all sides by updated remodels—their safe, traditional stance slowly but surely lowering their value.

In the United States alone, over six million start-ups are launched annually.[1] Google, Comcast, Amazon, Cisco, and Oracle are well-established Fortune 100 companies, yet none of them were on that list ten years ago. Twitter, Facebook, YouTube, and Pinterest connect billions of people around the globe. All were founded within the last decade.

This turbulence naturally impacts employment and careers. The conventional map of success—get a degree, start at the bottom, network aggressively, follow the rules, climb the ladder, retire comfortably—is now a no-man's-land.

The average adult worker in the United States holds more than 10 jobs in a lifetime.[2] It's become increasingly common to hold more than one job at a time, to reeducate yourself continuously and to reinvent your career three to four times. The simple inquiry "what do you do?" has become a complex question unanswerable with a simple title or function.

This chaotic landscape of constant and continual change is at odds with the established view of business and business leaders, particularly CEOs. Good CEOs once ruled from a position of stability. They commanded forces of people, money,

64% of SXSW attendees say they go to find new opportunities.

Buck, Stephanie. "SXSW by the Numbers." Mashable. Mar. 2013.

distribution networks, and brand imagery, bolting them together into a profit-making, market-share-gaining machine. An industry might be cutthroat, but it was understandable and advanced relatively slowly. Innovations required years of development. Aspiring CEOs wrote five-year business plans, built brand equity, assembled their associations, and climbed up a well-defined hierarchy.

The Rate of Change

| 1937 | 75 Yrs |
| Today | 15 Yrs |

In 1937, companies listed in the Standard & Poor's 500 had an average life expectancy of 75 years. Today, companies listed in Standard & Poor's 500 have an average life expectancy of just 15 years.

Hagel, John. "Running Faster, Falling Behind: John Hagel III on How American Business Can Catch Up." Knowledge@Wharton. 2010.

As attractive and permanent as that world may sound, it simply doesn't exist anymore and it isn't coming back.

We live in a time where little is predictable. No career path is predetermined. No one can play it safe. The majority of companies, their employees, and their leaders navigate a space where competitors appear overnight, customers demand innovations monthly, business plans rarely last a full year, and career ladders have been replaced by trampolines. This environment of incessant, non-linear change will only accelerate in the future. Traditional CEOs are ill-equipped to survive.

Only 1 in 4 employees believe their organizations have the leaders to succeed in the future.

Burke, Eugene and Glennon, Ray. 2012. The SHL Talent Report.

DESIGN

We're not the only ones to see this leadership gap.

In 2010, the IBM Global CEO Study announced, "More than rigor, management discipline, integrity or even vision—successfully navigating an increasingly complex world will require creativity." Two years later, it added three more essential traits: "empowering employees through values, engaging customers as individuals, and amplifying innovation through partnerships."[3]

Daniel Pink takes a holistic perspective and relabels our era the "conceptual age." As a result, CEOs need to be storytellers, big-picture thinkers, and empathetic humorists capable of giving meaning to our lives through their products, services, and management styles—not to mention their honest, revealing, re-tweetable posts.

Thomas Friedman warns that we're living in a hot, flat world where a successful CEO must upload, outsource, and offshore. Tom Kelley and David Kelley invite us to reclaim our creative confidence, while Sheryl Sandberg instructs us to "lean in."

Some authors and advisors focus attention on the problems, noting that today's challenges are "wicked" and defy conventional solutions. CEOs, we're told, need to change their character and develop peripheral vision, pattern recognition, an experimental mindset, and a high panic threshold.

A logical response to these avalanches of advice is to surrender. We throw up our hands and hope our inherent traits or some measure of luck will suffice. Perhaps we'll work for the right startup, or get the attention of the right boss, or happen upon the right industry in its earliest stages. Maybe we'll stumble across a mentor who can help us make sense of conflicting paths and tortuous routes.

Another response—the one advocated in this book—is to identify the business function best suited to these tumultuous times and use it to guide your actions. The business world has done this before. When companies needed to develop procedural discipline, it turned to Operations as a guide. When companies needed to attract and retain customers, Marketing led the way. When companies needed to learn how to scale, Finance provided the tools and perspective.

Now that companies need agility and imagination, in addition to analytics, we believe it's time to turn to Design as a model of leadership.

If you want to start a contentious, circular debate among a group of sophisticated, otherwise mature adults, ask them to define "design" as a business function. Google lists over four billion entries. Wikipedia adopts a particularly lame dictionary definition: "Design is the creation of a plan or convention for the construction of an object or a system (as in architectural blueprints, engineering drawings, business processes, circuit diagrams and sewing patterns)," then makes it worse by adding that no real definition exists.

The International Council of Societies of Industrial Design gives it credit for creativity, but then complicates it with grandiosity: "Design is a creative activity whose aim is to establish the multi-faceted qualities of objects, processes, services and their systems in whole life cycles. Therefore, design is the central factor of innovative humanisation of technologies and the crucial factor of cultural and economic exchange." Phew. Good to know.

A more recent definition from proponents of design thinking emphasizes design as problem solving that creates new, useful products, places, communications, or experiences. We have no argument with this description as long as problem solving is understood to be a process and not the literal definition of design (surely we can build on successes or enhance desires as well as solve problems). We would add—with emphasis—to design is to encourage collective change.

When we think *design*, our first association is *change*: change that responds to need, embodies desire, pursues a stated direction, and reflects a shared vision. Those who are designers—either through training or by nature—actively encourage and support collective change.

Historically, design changed "things." More recently it's changed services and interactions. Looking ahead it will change companies, industries, and countries. Perhaps it will eventually change the climate and our genetic code.

Leaders who understand this transformative role of design and embrace its traits and tenets can command in times of change. We call these leaders DEOs—Design Executive Officers—and they are our new heroes.

FROM CEO TO DEO

Ask a recruiter to describe the characteristics of a traditional CEO.

She'll first mention the need for an MBA and the disciplined financial perspective that degree implies. Nearly 40 percent of current CEOs add "MBA" to their collection of capitalized initials.[4] Next, she'll list traits associated with military commanders: authoritative, strategic, able to delegate, decisive, prepared to lead, equipped with a big-picture perspective. Finally, she'll suggest that the ideal CEO has some humanistic touches as well: personable, charismatic, perhaps a dash of compassion.

These traits have served companies well over the past century. When assembly lines traversed the Midwest and shift workers numbered in the tens of millions, CEOs made decisions and met deadlines. When most employees were low skilled or "cogs in a wheel," companies needed a commander at the top. They implemented order and ensured conformity.

And then the world changed.

We leaped out of the Industrial Age and buried our noses in the Information Age. By the time we looked up from our screens, we were advancing on the Conceptual Age and the business leadership traits we previously praised had started to weaken. They'd become a little creaky. They strained to be relevant.

If we could borrow Harry Potter's invisibility cape, we'd use it to visit an executive board meeting chaired by a traditional CEO. We'd see that he follows an agenda set months before. He points to data from the past quarter. He calls on each department to report on prescribed topics. Cloaked in invisibility, we'd slip outside and wander down the hall. In a cubicle, we'd find a young manager surreptitiously checking his social networks, future stock prices, competitors' posts, and more appealing job openings—all updated instantly in the palm of his hand.

This scenario is repeated all around the world where the gap between who the CEO is equipped to manage and who actually works for him or her grows wider by the day. Employees are increasingly higher skilled. They seek challenge and growth over security and predictability. They're networked both inside and outside their companies. Many have direct contact with customers. They've grown up collaborating and iterating in school and in personal relationships. They expect leadership that understands and embraces all this.

Putting a traditional CEO at the front of a modern workforce is anachronistic. He or she is the

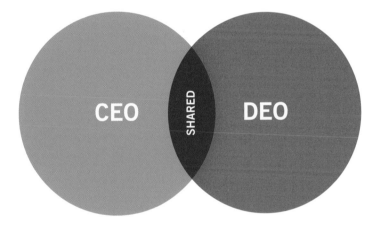

CEO TRAITS	SHARED TRAITS	DEO TRAITS
Top executive	**Ambitious**	Most senior partner
Authoritative	**Confident**	Aspirational
Linear thinker	**Rational**	Systems thinker
Executes to plan	**Competitive**	Experiments and improvises
Maintains stability and order		Permits useful disruption
Commands respect		Earns respect
Must be accurate		Comfortable with ambiguity
Delegates actions		Hands-on when needed
One-way communication		Networked
Follows the manual		Adapts and iterates as needed
Doesn't like to fail		Learns from mistakes
Sensitive to threats		Open to new experiences

Organizational Challenges

Leadership is the biggest people-side issue in organizations.

Freedman, Joshua. Feb 2012. 2012 Workplace Issues Report.

58% LEADERSHIP

24% TEAM PERFORMANCE

13% SALES

5% CUSTOMER SERVICE

outdated, boxy TV in an era of flat screens, the heavy-hulled yacht struggling to keep up in the America's Cup.

How do we fill this gap? Do we put traditional CEOs on steroids or add bionic components? Do we decide that women are better suited to the job or minorities or recent immigrants? Do we declare the job irrelevant and banish it altogether?

We suggest a simpler solution. Just as we took our cues from MBAs and the military in casting the ideal CEO of the 20th century, we can look to designers—in that term's broadest definition— to model our future leader, the DEO.

Proposing design-inspired leadership as the answer may sound delusional to some, like a zealous art teacher attacking poverty with a new color palette. But that's a knee-jerk reaction, based largely on associations of design with discretion, luxury, and logos. A more realistic assessment confirms that design leaders usually possess characteristics, behaviors, and mindsets that enable them to excel in unpredictable, fast-moving, and value-charged conditions.

With these traits, DEOs attract and coalesce stakeholders who share their vision, goals, and values. They build corporate cultures that nurture and retain talented employees. They lead teams who learn from one another and collaborate easily and effectively. With these traits, DEOs create resilient organizations that value expertise but make room for failure—organizations able to iterate and evolve with the changes taking place all around them.

For years, business acumen and creative ability have been siloed, united only at office parties and the occasional brainstorming session. But we live in a time that requires new leadership. We live in a time that requires people who look at every business challenge as a design problem solvable with the right mix of imagination and metrics.

1 Fairlie, Robert W. 2012. *Kauffman Index of Entrepreneurial Activity, 1996–2011.* http://www.kauffman.org/uploadedFiles/KIEA_2012_report.pdf
2 Bialik, Carl. "Seven Careers in a Lifetime?" Wall Street Journal, September 4, 2010. http://online.wsj.com/article/SB10001424052748704206804575468162805877990.html
3 IBM Global Business Services. 2012. Leading Through Connections: Insights from the IBM Global Chief Executive Officer Study. http://www.ibm.com/ceostudy2012
4 Spencer, Stuart. *2004 CEO Study: A Statistical Snapshot of Leading CEOs.*

Six defining characteristics of a DEO

Change Agents

DEOs aren't troubled by change; in fact, they openly promote and encourage it. They understand traditional approaches, but are not dominated by them. As a result, they are comfortable disrupting the status quo if it stands in the way of their dream. They try to think and act differently than others. They recognize this ability as a competitive advantage.

Risk Takers

DEOs embrace risk as an inherent part of life and a key ingredient of creativity. Rather than avoiding or mitigating it, they seek greater ease and command of it as one of the levers they can control. They recast it as experimentation and invite collaborators. A failed risk still produces learning.

Systems Thinkers

Despite their desire to disrupt and take risks, DEOs are systems thinkers who understand the interconnectedness of their world. They know that each part of their organization overlaps and influences another. They know unseen connections surround what's visible. This helps to give their disruptions intended, rather than chaotic, impact and makes their risk taking more conscious.

Intuitive

DEOs are highly intuitive, either by nature or through experience. They have the ability to feel what's right, by using their intense perceptual and observational skills or through deep expertise. This doesn't mean they have a fear of numbers. They know that intuitively enhanced decision making doesn't preclude rational or logical analysis. They use both—and consider each valid and powerful.

Socially Intelligent

DEOs have high social intelligence. They instinctively connect with others and integrate them into well-defined and heavily accessed networks. They prefer spending time with employees, customers, and strangers rather than equipment, plants, or spreadsheets. "Everyday people" are a source of strength, renewal, and new ideas.

GSD

Finally, DEOs can be defined by a new set of initials: GSD—short for "gets shit done." They feel an urgency to get personally involved, to understand details through their own interaction, and to lead by example. DEOs make things happen.

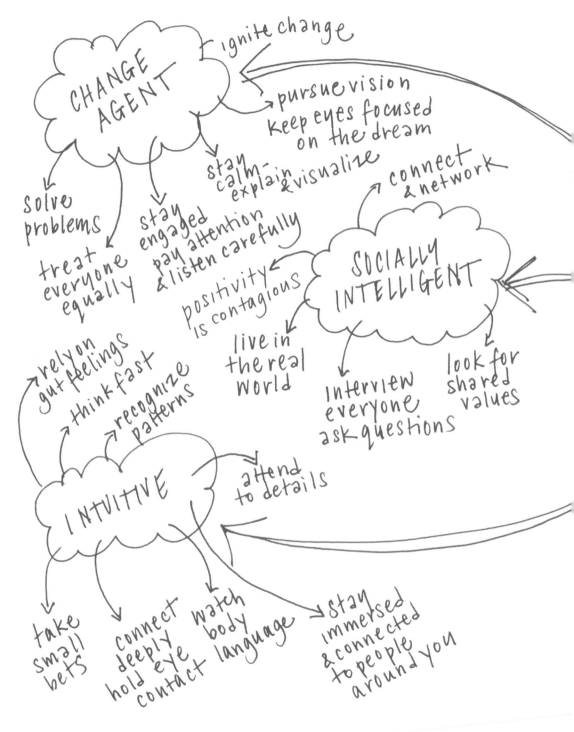

CHANGE AGENT

ignite change

pursue vision
keep eyes focused
on the dream

stay calm–
explain & visualize

solve problems

treat everyone equally

stay engaged
pay attention
& listen carefully

positivity
is contagious

connect & network

SOCIALLY INTELLIGENT

rely on gut feelings

think fast

recognize patterns

live in the real world

interview everyone
ask questions

look for shared values

INTUITIVE

attend to details

take small bets

connect deeply
hold eye contact

watch body language

stay immersed
& connected
to people
around you

risk = experimentation

RISK TAKER

failure to act is the larger risk

risk takers ≠ risk seekers

ask "why" not just how

understand processes, not just structure

risk collaborators frees people

smart risk explores new ground.

SYSTEMS THINKER

connect the dots

don't strip out buffer time

learn about motivation & hidden influences

track macro forces - watch for trends

me

the balance of dreaming with doing

make things happen

prioritize, 80/20 rule

GSD

too much is as damaging as too little

scan for the meat

just get started

what's the deadline

create a to-do list

CHANGE AGENT

It's one thing to be comfortable with change; it's another to actively promote and encourage it. When we say a DEO is a change agent, we mean that she is a catalyst, an influence that sparks transformation and brings about the conditions for change.

Sometimes this change is within a narrow sphere, for example, company culture. Marissa Meyer is attempting this at Yahoo!, where she has introduced perks such as free food, while insisting employees be present in the offices more often. Sometimes a DEO seeks broader change, revising business practices or even an entire industry. Ray Anderson did this after having a "spear in the heart" realization that his carpet company, Interface, was polluting the environment. He radically altered his company's production processes, prompting many corporations to rethink how they make and sell their products.

A few DEOs have the authority and visibility to change entire countries. Bill Clinton used his presence on the world stage to create the Clinton Global Initiative, a nonpartisan organization that convenes international leaders to collectively devise innovative solutions to humanity's most pressing problems. A central tenet of the initiative is each member's pledge to take new, specific, and measurable action that sets the conditions for positive change.

In each of these cases, the DEO ignites change, influencing and encouraging others to join in.

The change is not forced or mandated and it's not dependent on extraordinary charisma. Instead, a DEO uses characteristics and approaches proven to ease transitions.[1] She counts on trusted, supportive relationships with key stakeholders. She empathizes with those experiencing change as a phenomenon they don't control. She presents a clear plan and is open to feedback. She fuels change with her energy and optimism.

For a DEO, change is not something to fear—nor is it the main point of what she does. Change is simply what happens when she pursues a vision. Look at any successful DEO and you'll find a vision or dream choreographing the transformations she attempts. That guiding dream remains central to her activities and plans. It's the true north by which she adjusts the company's progress. It's the magnetic force pulling her toward the future and increasing her restless dissatisfaction with the status quo.

72% of employees surveyed said the ability to look ahead is the most important leadership trait

Kouzes, James and Posner, Barry Z. 2009. "To Lead, Create a Shared Vision," *Harvard Business Review*.

> **"**
> # Change is not merely necessary to life—it is life.
> ## Alvin Toffler
> **"**

For a DEO, the dreams that drive change are always entangled with the real world. These are not starry imaginings with no basis in day-to-day reality. Any vision worthy of driving an organization is well framed and succinctly defined. Constraints and hurdles are identified. Whether she's dissatisfied with the current situation or sees an opportunity that others miss, a DEO does more than just imagine what she wants to create. She paints a compelling vision of the future, sets clear, attainable goals, and establishes reasonable, meaningful milestones.

An effective DEO then paves that visionary path with data and feedback. She thirsts for unbiased, unfiltered information about the consequences of her actions. She wants the hot, the cold, the bitter, and the sweet. That taste—the experience of how change impacts everyone's "now"—helps her course correct and refine her company's trajectory. This responsive approach helps make change less frightening and more fruitful for her team. It gives credence to her leadership and confidence to her followers. She may be leading through uncharted territory, but she uses her community as a GPS and their shared vision as a map.

After years of introducing others to all levels of change, from the smallest tweak to the biggest rethink, a DEO's change agent skill set is well-honed and worth emulating.

Stay elevated

Change generates a smorgasbord of tantalizing, tasty details that can detract from the main meal. To counterbalance this diversion, a DEO keeps everyone's eyes focused on the dream, the vision, the higher value of change. She doesn't ignore tactical or functional elements of transitions, but continually provides higher-level guidance that makes those tasks more tolerable and significant.

For a DEO, this guidance depends on stakeholder buy-in to the vision. It gains refinement from feedback and gathers strength over time. Eventually, the DEO is not the only one proclaiming the company's aspirations. It becomes a future everyone envisions and passionately builds.

Stay flat

A DEO uses hierarchy strategically, not to stroke the egos of those in charge, but rather to increase knowledge sharing, collaboration, mentoring, and efficiency. Her preference for a relatively flat, modular organizational structure—similar in its design to the cells of organic systems— makes it easier to propose, activate, and assess change. Rather than accept rigid departments or isolated business units, a DEO seeks to create a honeycomb structure where key functional units are autonomous, yet interconnected and fully integrated in the whole.

Cellular organizations are easy to propose in theory and difficult to manage in reality unless authority, accountability, and recognition are fairly distributed. An effective DEO takes pains to put everyone on an equal level, to insist that it's not "me," but "we." She delegates power and responsibility in ways that directly benefit customers and stakeholders. She respects the independence of each unit, but constantly works to keep everyone united around the company's vision and values.

Stay engaged

By staying engaged in all the messy human details of a company, a DEO can clarify confusion and build trust. By understanding people's psychology and biases, she learns how to introduce change in a less disruptive way. By carefully listening to their stories, she learns where others may be open to change and where they are shut off.

This engagement and understanding extends from the organization to the rest of the world. A DEO thirsts for new information and has a constant appetite for learning. Rather than referring to Twitter as a "fire hose" or declaring "big data" overwhelming, a DEO tests ways of filtering information to make it more manageable and useful. She integrates learning into her daily ritual, making it as common as brushing her teeth or checking her email. If a day goes by when she doesn't learn something new, she adds another resource to her newsfeed, scans for local meetups she can join, or finds a new book to download.

Stay calm

Ask people to describe a designer or creative person and they will likely include the term "emotional." The assumption is that to be creative is to be freely expressive and stripping out that quality leaves a designer neutered and impotent. Hardly.

A DEO knows that the fastest route to spreading change is to explain it. Some DEOs do this in a logical, rational manner that makes clear why the change is needed and how the new solution will work. Others visualize the impact of change, illustrating what it will look like and feel like. Still others act as role models and coaches, demonstrating how to enjoy change. That's not to say emotion isn't needed, but it's added back into the argument as fuel, not direction.

---

1 Lunenburg, Fred C. 2010. "Managing Change: The Role of the Change Agent." International Journal of Management, Business and Administration, Vol. 13, No. 1.

Workouts to build your change agent-ness

Start small.

Start with minimal changes that impact you on a daily basis: Change how you arrange your clothes in your closet. Change where you store your kitchen utensils. Change your morning routine to include one new activity. Wear a new heel height or a new color or a new accessory. Put your watch on the opposite wrist. Read a book in a genre you've never tried before, like science fiction, history, or biology.

Shift perspective.

Work up to more central changes: Try maintaining a separate identity online (not to send naked pictures of yourself to co-eds—if you're doing that you need more help than we can provide). Introduce yourself to a stranger in a novel way, highlighting something new. Rewrite your LinkedIn profile to offer a different perspective on your career.

Lead change.

Graduate to "change agent in training" status: Offer to lead a new project that will require you to learn something. Draft a plan to introduce a new product for your company (even if that's not your job). Start moonlighting in a different career or create a startup that you work on each morning before you go to your day job.

Watch yourself.

Track your emotional state for a few weeks after making a change that seems significant to you. Notice slight improvements in your mood over time as you become more accustomed to your new situation. Understanding this pattern of initial emotional discomfort or resistance followed predictably by improvement can help ease your next change.

GO DEEPER

Who Moved My Cheese by Spencer Johnson
Switch: How to Change Things When Change is Hard by Chip Heath and Dan Heath
Change by Design by Tim Brown
Leading Change by John P. Kotter
Mindset by Carol S. Dweck

RISK TAKER

Thanks to the financial catastrophes and political misfortunes of the last decade, risk taking has become associated with rogue bankers, deceitful investors, and philandering governors. By these standards, to be a risk taker is to court disaster. But DEOs take risks because creativity demands it.

There is no innovation, no true originality, without some measure of risk. A new song, a more efficient car, a more effective vaccine—the category doesn't matter. Every success is the result of risk taking at some point.

According to Harvard Business School professor Clayton Christensen, 30,000 new consumer products are launched each year and 95 percent of them fail. Vegas offers better odds. And yet a good DEO knows that failure to act is the larger risk. When everything around is changing, standing still doesn't protect from failure; in fact, it ensures failure. If a racer stays put once the starting gun sounds, he's guaranteed last place.

In some instances, taking a risk may be the only competitive advantage a DEO has. When skill, experience, and assets are roughly equal, the winning difference can be a matter of who takes the right risk.

Success Requires Risk

In most sports and other competitive ventures, success is a combination of skill, training and risk.

Schwalbe, Michael. 2013. "The 40-30-30 Rule: Why Risk is Worth It."

RISK — 30%

SKILL — 30%

40%

TRAINING

Because a DEO needs risk, he befriends it. He spends time understanding how it works and when it makes the most sense to pursue it. With experience, his ability to accurately assess risk improves, as does his estimation of its consequences.[1] Over time, risk loses its edge and instead becomes a familiar business ingredient, an acknowledged element of every decision.

In developing risk muscle, a DEO works to find the balance between fear-dominated inertia and foolhardy gambling. The optimal risk posture is not a static position, but rather an iterative, ongoing journey between choices that are too safe and ones that end in failure. Course correcting through levels of risk may sound like a setup for whiplash or at least nausea. A DEO reduces that perceived volatility for himself and his colleagues by recasting risk as experimentation.

Turning risk into research means every risk a DEO takes will result in new insights and greater experience, regardless of the outcome. This simple shift in perspective, highlighting the inherent value of trying something new, smooths the zigzag path of iteration into an upward curve of increasing capability and confidence.

Of course, terminology alone doesn't turn risk into experimentation. An experiment follows a structure. When taking a risk, a DEO

does the same. He starts with a hypothesis or a well-articulated framework that guides the risk taking. This beginning clarifies the nature of the risk and makes it easier to accurately assess. Next, the DEO identifies influences and other factors—including luck—that may affect the outcome. Ideally, some type of control variable is available for comparison.

A clear hypothesis and awareness of variables helps stakeholders share in the risk taking and accept it as reasonable experimentation. Contingency plans, adequate supervision, progress monitoring and limited duration help coordinate efforts and calm nerves.

When the results are in, the risk may be over but the experiment continues. The DEO gains support for his risk taking by always conducting a post-mortem that not only identifies wins or losses, but also recognizes and shares what the company learned.

This approach to risk taking as careful, directed experimentation ensures progress, while reducing the chance of irretrievable failure. Assuming it's sized, shared, and rewarded appropriately, it helps a DEO claim the competitive advantage that smart risk taking offers.

Size the risk

Big companies can usually afford to take larger risks than small companies. That seems like a no-brainer, but sadly, it's not. Often the size of the risk matches the size of the leader's ego.

DEOs are risk takers, but they're not risk seekers. Risk seekers try to defy the odds, often betting on luck or talent not readily visible to those around them. They tend to "bet the house" on win-lose propositions, leaving themselves no middle ground or Plan B.

In contrast, DEOs know their company's appetite and tolerance for risk and set boundaries accordingly. The bets they take are often grounded on solid data and deep insight. They're not counting on luck, although they're quick to welcome it if it shows up. DEOs can make big bets, but they're more comfortable experimenting in small increments with an alternate Plan B waiting in the wings if needed. This diligence reassures everyone that risk taking and the company's well being aren't at odds.

"

Only those who risk going too far can possibly find out how far they can go.
T.S. Eliot

"

Share the risk

The worst risks to take are those taken alone, without the counsel or support of others. While including others in risk taking is time consuming and often contentious, DEOs know that it increases their chance of success. Diverse perspectives contribute to a better definition and keener assessment of what's at stake.

Partners can also help extend risk taking into more areas. Numerous studies have found that risk taking is domain specific, meaning that comfort with taking a risk in one area doesn't necessarily transfer to another. While a DEO may jump to take creative chances, he may balk at financial risks. Similarly, he may feel confident betting on an American market, but be hesitant to gamble on a Chinese market. Risk collaborators with complementary expertise can fill these voids.

This recognition of risk taking as a joint venture also frees people from the panic of personal failure. It helps individuals contribute ideas, suggestions, connections, or cautions. Knowing that participation does not equal blame opens the door to increased creativity.

Reward the risk

Finally, DEOs reward risk taking, regardless of the outcome. They champion it in themselves and those who work with them, not only when the risk works but also when it doesn't. They acknowledge failures in the same way they acknowledge successes—as the result of collaboration and a shared desire to move forward.

This doesn't mean a DEO champions any risk, distributing praise like cheap "Good Job!" trophies. He rewards smart risk taking that builds on previous learning and explores new ground. He salutes effective risk takers as people who push forward, relentlessly searching for ways to enhance or advance the company.

---

1 Warrell, Margie. 2013. *Stop Playing Safe*. Milton, Australia: John Wiley & Sons.

Workouts to build risk-taking ability

Take steps.

As with making change, it's best to start with minimal risks where failure isn't life threatening. Identify a small personal fear and try to conquer it. Your small but notable risk might be singing karaoke or riding a Ferris wheel or telling a joke. Reward yourself each time you take these chances—even if you don't succeed in overcoming the fear. Rinse and repeat until the risk seems minimal.

Play games.

Strategy games are an effective exercise in risk taking. Sign up for online versions or buy the old-school board games. Checkers, chess, Risk, Monopoly, Civilization, World of Warcraft, and dozens of other choices simulate real-world risk taking within an abstract or fantasy world. Add in money and increase the realism.

Tag along.

Join a team that seems more comfortable at risk taking than you are and force yourself to keep up. This can be at work or at play, but if it involves your head, wear a helmet.

Build buffers.

Buffers, like having extra money in the bank or a second job, can raise your risk-taking aptitude by lowering the consequences of failure. Examine your reasons for avoiding risks and find a way to compensate for them.

GO DEEPER

Against the Gods: The Remarkable Story of Risk by Peter L. Bernstein
Chaos: Making a New Science by James Gleick
The Wisdom of Crowds by James Surowiecki
Little Bets: How Breakthrough Ideas Emerge from Small Discoveries by Peter Sims

SYSTEMS THINKER

In the simplest terms, systems thinking is the ability to understand connections. It's the recognition that much of what occurs around us is the result of linked systems that influence one another, often in subtle ways. DEOs learn this skill early and use it habitually.

Traditionally an aptitude of engineers, economists, and other highly analytic professionals, systems thinking has spread more broadly to boardrooms, cubicles, and collaboration spaces. The practice that started out as a neatly diagrammed process sketched on hundreds of engineering classroom blackboards has become an everyday tool of DEOs.

Systems thinking helps us deal with the increasing complexity of the world. This mode of thinking goes beyond the cause-and-effect of linear thinking where A causes B and fixing A fixes B.

A systems thinker views everything as an ecosystem where A might affect B, L, X, and sometimes Z. Fixing A might fix B, but doing so might also make L and X worse. Systems thinking accepts that events may result from patterns of behavior, underlying relationships or mental models that are not always evident and may seem unrelated.

A story chronicled by Steven Levitt and Stephen Dubner in their book, *Freakonomics,* illustrates how influences and outcomes of a system are rarely obvious except in hindsight. The nation thought the decision on Roe v. Wade fixed the problem of illegal abortions, but it turns out to have done much more. Legalizing abortions saved millions of women from unwanted pregnancies. The reduction of unwanted pregnancies decreased the number of children born into poverty. This decrease lowered the criminal population (because living in poverty raises the likelihood of criminal behavior) and consequently decreased the country's crime rate—20 years after the Supreme Court decision. At this point, any systemic thinking about abortion must include not only the question of when life begins, but also the question of how crime ends.

Not all problems are as gnarled and interwoven as Roe v. Wade, but most have more than a simple linear framework. Systems thinking strives to ascertain root causes and leverage points, so that any intervention heals the system as a whole without unintended consequences. Systems thinkers may not be able to avoid all surprises, but they hope to reduce them or at least do a better job anticipating them.

Designers often have refined systems thinking ability. They're trained to understand that the whole is greater than the sum of its parts and that small elements can radically alter an experience. They typically have astute pattern recognition skills and an almost instinctual ability to find leverage points.

Designers—and those who learn from them—are able to think in metaphors and use models

Unseen Influences

REACT
Events
What happened?

ANTICIPATE
Patterns & Trends
What has been happening?

DESIGN
Systemic Structures
What are the forces at play contributing to these patterns?

TRANSFORM
Mental Models
What about our thinking allows this situation to persist?

Systems thinking accepts that events may result from patterns of behavior, underlying relationships, or mental models that are not always evident and may seem unrelated.

to explore connections and networks. They learn to iterate in small ways, by adding or removing elements to see what happens before making wholesale change. They crave feedback and quickly deduce the importance of context.

A DEO applies systems thinking skills to create and build her company as well as its offerings. She consciously regards her company as an ecosystem, striving to understand its interlocking connections. She also recognizes that some developments may only come through trial and error because their consequences are non-intuitive and hard to predict. Free breakfast raises overhead costs, but more than offsets that expense by increasing productivity. A new time-tracking system accurately logs labor, but impedes collaboration. A manager's unfunded, offbeat side project results in a viral video that draws millions of new viewers to a company's website.

An appreciation of system interdependency and the likelihood of unintended or unforeseen consequences leads a DEO to constantly ask why something works as it does and not just how. This perspective leads to habits that help highlight and spread systems thinking throughout the organization.

Connect the dots

DEOs look for the connective tissue between departments, projects, people, and any other elements of their business. They try to understand the processes that generate results rather than the structure. They recognize that everything is related to the big picture and that a broken system impacts more than itself.

To gain further insights into these types of interdependencies, DEOs become students of behavioral science, seeking to learn all they can about motivation and hidden influences. Fortunately, this field of study attracts practitioners with good social skills and fine writing abilities. Behavioral scientists are rapidly assuming celebrity status in the business world, jostling with economists and entrepreneurs for top billing at conferences and top book rankings on Amazon or Barnes & Noble.

Use the Force

DEOs with well-developed systems thinking skills respect the power of natural forces to help them achieve their goals. By studying a system's dynamics—how and why it works—DEOs find leverage points where the system can naturally support or subvert change. By keeping abreast of trends, DEOs have the equivalent of a jetpack to fuel future endeavors.

Tom LaForge, Coca-Cola's Global Director of Human and Cultural Insights, suggests focusing on two powerful conduits of change. He tracks macro forces like Internet connectivity and demographics that are certain to have broad impact. He also watches for emerging cultural trends that are more variable and have regional impact. Monitoring these two powerful influences help development teams anticipate future conditions that could impede or propel their work.

Take the time

Systems thinkers know that the best solutions are rarely quick reactions—they take time to germinate. There are a host of details and interrelationships to consider, many of which might get worked out in a less conscious part of the brain. Creating breaks in the timeline and letting the problem "stew" for a while raises the chance of success.

In contrast to lean development models now popular in entrepreneurial circles, DEOs caution their teams against stripping the buffer time from a project. Unless they fear an audit by Congress, they'll spring for the sports outing or corporate dance lessons because they understand the profound benefit of unstructured activities and downtime.

Workouts to build systems thinking

Take turns.

Systems thinking skills benefit from contextual knowledge and hands-on experience. You'll understand a system better if you interact with it directly. Try changing jobs with someone at work for a day, and then compare notes on what could be improved. Learn an activity that requires relationship. Dancing with a partner is a good choice.

Change places.

You can change your perspective on anything you're studying and see it in a different way. If you're reading a report online, print it out. If you're conducting a meeting in a conference room, move it outside. If you're taking a client out to lunch, change the venue to a museum. This new perspective often reveals hidden parts of a system. A common trick to change perspective on a company is to pretend you've been hired as its new leader. What changes would you make?

Borrow stuff.

Don't be shy when it comes to borrowing from others—systems often share common behaviors despite their disparities. Start collecting patterns and models of behavior. These can help you understand and address new problems quickly. For example, if you have a method of increasing trust in a group, you can extend that model online to a much larger cohort. If you have a trick for breaking the ice at a party, you might be able to apply that to new employee orientations.

Draw lines.

Learn to diagram and use this skill to increase your understanding of system interactions. Diagrams can deconstruct everything from sentences to nuclear power plants. An easy first step is to learn to make schematic drawings with lines, arrows, circles, and squares.

GO DEEPER

Thinking in Systems: A Primer by Donella H. Meadows
Business Dynamics: Systems Thinking and Modeling for a Complex World by John Sterman
The Fifth Discipline: The Art and Practice of the Learning Organization by Peter Senge
Emergence: The Connected Lives of Ants, Brains, Cities, and Software by Steven Johnson
Out of Control: The New Biology of Machines, Social Systems, and the Economic World by Kevin Kelly
Freakonomics by Steven Levitt and Stephen Dubner

Carl Bass

President and CEO of Autodesk

Carl's presence fills any room he enters, not because his ego pushes others out, but because his demeanor welcomes and connects with everyone around him. In title, he is the president and CEO of Autodesk, a $2 billion corporation that creates 3-D design software that's used around the world. In practice, he's a DEO.

We interviewed Bass on a sunny afternoon in the Berkeley shop he shares with a friend. Surrounded by traditional woodworking implements, repurposed discards, and a state-of-the-art robotic lathe, he explained how he built his career and crafted his life.

As a child, what did you think you'd be when you grew up?

I don't think I spent any time as a kid thinking about what I wanted to be. I never thought, "I'm going to be a fireman." I've always just done what's most interesting in front of me. It was more of a meander. There was nothing purposeful about it.

When I first went to college, I only went for a brief time and decided I hated it. So I dropped out and ended up in South Dakota. I was just driving across the country with a friend and we ran out of money somewhere near Wounded Knee. I stayed for about a year on the Indian reservation, building houses and learning how to do carpentry.

Next, I wandered over to Seattle. I kind of poked my nose into a woodshop there and asked, "Can I come and sweep up the chips or something in exchange for using your shop space?" That's where I taught myself how to make stuff. Then I apprenticed with a blacksmith. Next, I learned to build boats and furniture. I finally went back to college, but I spent probably five, six, maybe even seven years exploring and wandering between when I started and when I finished.

When did you discover your creative side?

I've always tried to figure out connections. That's how I think of creativity and that's the common thread that runs through everything

I do. Whether it's a design problem or a math problem or anything else I do at work, it's all about solving a problem or a challenge by figuring out the connections and working within some constraint. You're trying to figure out an answer. Math is exactly that. Design is that. And business has a huge aspect of doing that. You have a whole bunch of constraints and within those constraints you try to find a reasonable answer. That's my sense of creativity.

When did you first realize you could lead?

I'm a reluctant executive. I never wanted to be a CEO. I don't understand someone who just wants to be a business executive and so they move from company to company to rise up the ladder. I don't understand that motivation.

There are many parts of the job I don't particularly like, so I've surrounded myself with people who are good at the things I don't like doing. I've always tried to find the people who enjoy doing the stuff that I don't like doing.

How has your leadership style evolved?

I think I started as a more heroic leader, where I was going to try to lead the charge and solve the problem. But in a big company, the leader can't do the work himself. I can't pull together six smart people working really hard and run Autodesk. So over time, I've become much more collaborative, partly by conscious change—working with coaches and becoming more aware of my impact on people—and partly just by growing older.

Now I find myself a fair amount of time sitting at work thinking "I'm really here for my employees." I've become much more willing to discuss philosophical questions or show someone how

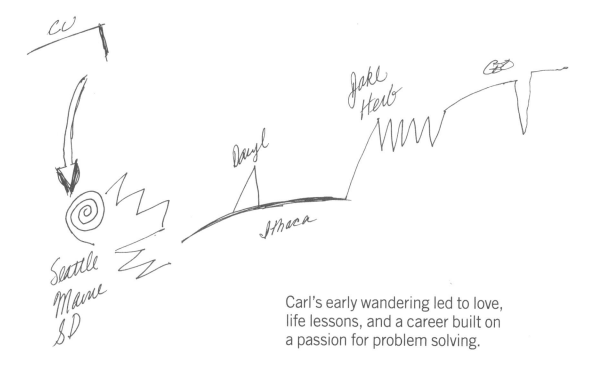

Carl's early wandering led to love, life lessons, and a career built on a passion for problem solving.

I've thought about a problem or give my perspective. I think it's a lot like being a parent: you learn to pass on knowledge and skills. They'll take what they want from me and get rid of much of it. But, you know, it's a way of influencing.

I used to only be interested in the work that people did. My attitude was kind of school of hard knocks. I was much more selfish with my time—I didn't want to waste it explaining stuff. If you're smart enough to get it, great; if not, too bad. I could be ridiculously critical and unashamed to say it. I didn't realize that if you care more about people, you get better work from them.

Over time you learn it's reasonable to care about people. People have careers. They have aspirations. They have stuff they want to accomplish. And having a little empathy for them doesn't kill you. If you invest in them early on, mentoring or teaching, the benefits of it are off the charts.

What do you love most about your job now?

The thing I love most is actually making new products. I like it when everything is new, and I get most interested in what kind of design problems we can solve, what experiences we can create. The second thing I love is meeting people who are actually using the products. It's really fun to see their creativity and imagination taking the product to different places.

You get this multiplicative effect when you hand a talented person a new tool, and they take it in this direction and you go, "Wow, I didn't even know that was possible!" Because of the diversity of the people who use our software—one day I'll be in Hollywood and the next day in Stuttgart—I get to work with some of the most creative people in the world.

Do you think innovation depends more on process or people?

It seems to me it always starts with getting the best people. There's almost no endeavor I can think of in which you don't benefit from having the best people. If you want the best design firm, if you want the most innovative company, if you want the best software, if you want the best NBA team, the first thing you do is go out and get the best people—people who are creative and smart and willing to break the rules and try different stuff.

The second thing is to build a culture that encourages and rewards risk and failure. I mean smart failure. As the head of an organization, you can't celebrate stupid failure. Say an employee comes to you and says, "I got a broken leg." And you ask, "How did you break your leg?" If he says, "Well, I was testing this gravity theory. So I jumped out the window," that's a stupid failure because there's a less risky way to do that.

But if you're always punishing people who take risks, the organization will see it clearly. If the only people who get ahead are the ones who sandbag their projects, who take the easier assignments that they're sure will succeed, it says to everybody else in the organization that this is the way to behave. I'd rather reward somebody who goes out and does something really hard and learns from it.

How do you lead in a time of change?

I think risk in innovation is the lifeblood of a company, particularly technology companies and, increasingly, all companies. Life spans are short. Things are changing quickly. You've got to change pretty rapidly. Yet in many ways, the bigger companies get, the more they're set up

to preserve themselves. The nature of the corporation is that there are a million forces that fight to preserve things as they are, or to at least continue in the same direction. There are very few forces inside a company that encourage you to do things differently.

Look at companies that didn't make it through transitions, like Kodak, Xerox, Lotus, Word-Perfect, and maybe now Yahoo! You wonder

> "
> # Risk in innovation is the lifeblood of a company.
> "

how Kodak could have possibly missed digital photography. They owned every patent. They owned all the technology. I don't think in any of these cases people were unaware of the changes around them. I don't think the people running them were stupid. So what went wrong in these companies?

I think it's the frame of reference that executives have around their business. They end up looking at the wrong things and then making the wrong decisions. For example, two years ago someone at Autodesk started speculating about consumers being interested in creativity and imagination and wanting to have tools to do this stuff. This guy says, "I think we could have a hundred million users of these things." Well, at that point we had a total of ten million users over all our years in business. It was one of those moments where if I'd had a megaphone I would have shouted, "You're an idiot!" The first application we were creating was this drawing app on an iPhone. Who wants to finger paint on a device that's this big?

But we went forward, and now we have about 135 million users of our consumer apps. The guy was not only right, he underestimated the size of the market. It would've been really easy to go down the Kodak route.

When it comes to the future, how do you know you're looking at the right things?

I ask that of us at Autodesk all the time. I say, "Are we missing the boat in some ways?" Right now, we're in this era where we're pushing very hard for cloud-based software for design. It's all cloud and it's all mobile, even though it's not what our customers buy today. I spend half my days thinking this is the most brilliant idea. I spend the other half of my days wondering why more people aren't doing it and if they are seeing something we aren't.

We did this really interesting strategy exercise where we told a bunch of people to go out and discover what the world of design, engineering, and creating products will look like in the future. People came back with all kinds of stuff. What was overwhelmingly interesting is that almost every story centered around who someone was going to work with and how they were going to get their work done.

As a company of self-admitted nerds, we had spent all our time thinking about how we're going to make better tools. If it's more realistic and it has more polygons, it's going to be even more awesome. And yet the insights we got from the strategy exercise were about the process, not the tools.

This completely changed the new product we're creating. Now the screen you spend the most time on looks something like Facebook, even though it's a design app. You log on in the morning and it's like a design feed, an activity stream,

that's all about what happened with the design. It's all about what people did. It's all about sharing stuff. And that came out of this exercise. It wasn't natural for us—we would've never gotten there on our own. It's only because someone said, "Before we go too crazy with this idea, why don't we just sit back? It's summertime, so let people dangle their feet in the water and think about it." The social component has become almost the largest component of the tools going forward. It just goes to show how teams of people can have big blind spots if they're not careful.

Do you have control over the corporate culture?

I think culture is one of those Zen things. You can't control it perfectly, but as the organization's leader you probably have the most control of anybody. And there's no doubt that every place has a culture, whether you consciously create it or not.

The leaders set the tone. I think in an organization, at every level, there are people who are perceived to be influential and powerful and organizations work to make them happy. So I'm going to model the things I want to see in others, and I'm going to try to accomplish what I expect in others. That's why I say it's Zen-like, in that you definitely control it, but it's not like the way you control a compensation policy or a sales quota or a development technique.

Culture also develops over time. It's subtle. Lots of things influence it. It's somewhat of a reflection. In our case, the culture lives out through 7,000 people behaving a certain way. And the 7,000 people aren't always the same— whoever was there on Friday, there'll be a slightly different set on Monday. A year from now, there'll be a different set of people. But there's a constancy to the way they act. And the way they act at Autodesk is different than a company upstairs or a company across the country.

The Autodesk Gallery showcases and explains the leading edge of technology in support of design, science, engineering, and entertainment.

Another cultural thread that runs through Autodesk is having greater empathy for what our customers do, how hard it is to do what they do, and the challenges they face. We have better appreciation for great designers, artists, and architects. I think there's more of this than when I started here. So I think you can change culture, but you change it very subtly and slowly.

The Autodesk Gallery is a celebrated space. What prompted you to create it?

Years ago I'd gone to a company in San Francisco called Esprit. It was a clothing company and they had a textile museum attached to their corporate headquarters. A friend dragged me there, but it turned out to be awesome. I realized we could create a design gallery at Autodesk. It's really hard to explain what we do at Autodesk. With the gallery we can show what goes on in the world of design, science, engineering, and entertainment.

When you're gone from the scene, what three things do you want to be known for?

One, I want to be known for solving problems well. Two, for helping people get their best work done. And three, for doing things that people hadn't thought of doing before.

INTUITIVE

We've all experienced the blessing of intuition. The sudden urge to double-check a departure time that saves us from missing a flight. The confidence to hire a candidate after only a 10-minute chat. The uneasy sense that something is misrepresented in a deadline-driven deal.

These common brushes with an unexplainable insight help explain why 62 percent of company leaders say they rely heavily on gut feelings or intuition when making a business decision.[1] We all have some measure of intuition functioning for us. DEOs employ it in force and work it overtime.

To be intuitive is to know something without necessarily being able to explain how or why we know it; to feel what's right or what may work.

Because of its vague genesis, intuition is often associated with the mystical or spiritual, instantly making it suspicious in business settings despite its role in top-level decision making.

Scientists, economists, psychologists, and management theorists have tried for decades to explain the process that allows people to synthesize highly complex information quickly and effectively with little rational thought. Some studies suggest that intuitive judgments are the result of intense perceptual and observational skills. Highly intuitive people may have a keener ability to see subtle but important details.

Other findings explain intuition as "fast thinking" that comes from years of study and experience. Experts become adept at pattern recognition within their area of competence and can rapidly make good judgments despite mind-numbing complexity.

A common debate pits intuition's value in business against its duller cousin, analysis. DEOs ignore this false dichotomy, knowing that intuitively enhanced decision making doesn't preclude rational or logical analysis. They use both—and consider each valid and powerful. A DEO can intuitively sense when something's wrong, then use assessment tools to figure out where the problem is. He can analyze broad opportunities in the market, then use intuition to discern elusive, but crucial specifics.

While the debate continues over how and why intuition happens, experts seem to agree that it's most useful in circumstances where speed or unconventional ideas are most needed—in other words, the environment in which DEOs operate every day.

"

It is by logic that we prove, but by intuition that we discover.
Henri Poincaré

"

62%

of leaders say they rely on their gut feelings when making decisions.

PRWeek/Burson-Marsteller CEO Survey, 2007.

Simply having intuitive skills doesn't make someone a DEO. After all, intuition can be used to avoid risk and run from change.

Intuitive abilities, under the command of a good DEO, can move a company forward. This means that the people surrounding a DEO must have a deep trust in his intuition. They may joke about the DEOs psychic powers, but they'll rarely bet against his perceptions.

DEOs earn this trust over time by sharing their intuition and using their "spidey sense" to take small bets. They're not embarrassed by their intuitive perceptions nor do they think it makes them immune from error. They freely acknowledge when they're operating on gut instinct, and they encourage pushback. They learn through trial and error when their intuition is really a bias or prejudice and when it's true perceptiveness. They publicly acknowledge when their intuition was wrong and attempt to understand why.

DEOs also appreciate and point out intuitive ability in others. They don't think they're the only ones with a sixth sense. In fact, they seek others with insight into areas where their own intuition is less adept. They encourage

Intuitive

Analytic

Intuitive	Analytic
Solutions can arrive very quickly	Requires time to do well
Best for problems that are well-understood	Best for problems that require research
Difficult to use when problem is complex	Can break down large, complex problems
Requires trust; solution is hard to replicate	Follows a process that others can duplicate

development of this sense as an accepted skill and don't automatically balk at exercises or training designed to enhance it.

Perhaps intuitive skills flow in unlimited quantity. Maybe, like other muscles, intuition needs to be strengthened through exercises like attending to details, connecting deeply, and staying immersed. DEOs prefer to think and act as though this were true because they have a hunch that it might be.

Attend to details

DEOs believe their intuition depends on an accurate awareness of environments, people, actions, and beliefs. That makes them pay very close attention to even the finest details. Since they don't know which detail is most important, they try to attend to the widest range possible.

This generates a barrage of questions, commonly starting with why. It means that no facet of a problem or presentation goes unquestioned. It means random conversations with musicians, jugglers, writers, taxi drivers, doormen, hair stylists, and, of course, bartenders. Everyone contributes a piece to the puzzle.

Connect deeply

Like details, personal connections fuel DEO perceptions. DEOs listen attentively. They hold eye contact. They watch body language. They lessen others' reservations with laughter and lore.

They consciously strive to sense others' feelings without filters or bias.

These deep connections are often the pathways over which a DEO's intuition flows. He quickly identifies which people accelerate and complement his intuitive sensibilities and keeps those people close. To a DEO, hell is a meeting of impersonal managers gathered to report on dry data to fill empty spreadsheets with no real purpose. The addition of at least one highly intuitive co-conspirator can change this meeting into a hunt for the hidden reason behind why the company never gets anything done.

Stay immersed

Delegation is an essential tool of business we're told, but it can separate a leader from important connections that can refine his intuitions. A DEO seeks to better understand how his company actually works. Who moves projects through processes? Who obsesses over how new customers learn about the company? Who can make problems go away and resources appear overnight?

While a DEO may not be able to do everyone's job, he strives to understand each department's responsibilities and contribution to the whole. This familiarity becomes a foundation on which his intuition can build.

1 PRWeek/Burson-Marsteller CEO Survey, 2007.

Workouts to become more intuitive

Go topless.

We often encourage people to "go topless," that is, laptop-less. We'll extend that encouragement to all computers, cell phones, game modules, and other electronic leashes that keep us firmly tied to the rational. Give yourself time each day to disconnect. In that time, reconnect with your intuitive self by daydreaming, wondering, meditating, or just musing.

Buy a round.

Cocktails or any drink that suggests playfulness can loosen the binds of the rational corset and provide some room for intuitive rumblings. We're not suggesting you bury yourself in a bottle, but any drink that sports an umbrella will probably lift your spirits and free up a few noteworthy thoughts.

Culture up.

The arts have long been associated with intuitive powers. Regular visits to museums, galleries, concert halls, and sculpture gardens can strengthen your intuitive infrastructure. Similarly, reading fiction or poetry, free-form dancing, singing, and any other celebration of non-work-related activities potentially carves new neural connections that might improve your intuition when you return to a more buttoned-up setting.

Chill out.

Meditation, yoga, soaking in hot tubs, and a host of behaviors recommended to reduce stress have the added advantage of increasing intuitive thinking. We're not sure if this is science or fiction, but it's pleasurable so why not try it?

GO DEEPER

Thinking, Fast and Slow by Daniel Kahneman
Blink: The Power of Thinking without Thinking by Malcolm Gladwell
Intuition: Its Powers and Perils by David Myers
Strategic Intuition: The Creative Spark in Human Achievement by William Duggan

DEOs believe that the success of a business lies in its people and their powerful, meaningful connections to one another. When stakeholders share a common vision and are aligned in their actions, they form a connective tissue that unites the company across departments, locations, and levels of seniority.

If you've ever visited a church where a passionate minister bonds his congregation in song, then you have a model of how potent and influential this behavior can be. Substitute Steve Jobs as the minister and Apple fans as the congregation and you have hard evidence of its power.

Meaningful connections synchronize effort and direction. A company's people become a unique and formidable asset that no competitor can imitate. A well-defined and tightly aligned collective of stakeholders attracts employees, clients, and partners who are a good fit for the company.

Meaningful interpersonal connections serve as a delivery system for the company's values, with each stakeholder expressing and communicating the company's principles. It adds to the company's resilience—its ability to withstand downturns. It's even been shown to increase productivity and profits.[1]

Developing this effective assemblage of talent and intent isn't easy. If it were, every company would have it. DEOs have the best odds of generating it not only because they recognize its value, but also because they are socially intelligent.

Social intelligence is the skill of navigating and negotiating complex social relationships and environments. It requires a clear and conscious self-awareness along with an appreciation of the broader definition of what it means to be human. It unites social awareness—traits such as empathy and perceptiveness—with social facility, the ability to work effectively in a group. It grows and deepens through direct connection with others.

DEOs connect with people so routinely that it becomes instinctual. Whether greeting a new hire, conversing with a customer, meeting with a partner, or welcoming the housekeeping staff, a DEO takes the time to connect, make eye contact, acknowledge the other person, and listen carefully to that person's message. A DEO easily forms rewarding relationships and comfortably extends her influence. This connection with others grounds her and builds her confidence to lead where there are no paved roads and few signposts.

A DEO's social intelligence can even infect her organization, raising levels of enthusiasm, happiness, creativity, excitement, calm, and a range of other affects. She accomplishes this partially through role modeling, but it's even more sophisticated and fundamental than that: a DEO's attitude is literally contagious.[2] A happy, outgoing, and socially intelligent DEO can change the emotions of those around her, increasing employees' performance, income, collaboration, and creativity.

EQ

Social Awareness
Empathy, attunement, accurate perceptions, and social cognition

+

Social Facility
The ability to work in sync with others, self presentation, influence and concern.

EQ signifies emotional intelligence, a conceptual measurement of the ability to relate to others.

Social Intelligence: The New Science of Social Relationships by Daniel Goleman. 2006.

Tag along with a DEO through a normal day and see how the contagion spreads as she interviews everyone, seeks diversity, and lives in the real world.

Interview everyone
A DEO thrives on personal connectivity. She uses it to gain valuable insight into beliefs, trends, biases, and bullshit. Her interactions go beyond her immediate colleagues and partners. She quizzes her teenage kids about politics, her elderly aunt about fashion, and her stylist about movies. Bartenders become her professors of behavioral science and cab drivers her economists. Every interaction is a potential goldmine of information.

To gain from these interactions, a DEO develops her interviewing skills beyond casual questioning. She learns to tease out details, to probe

"

A dream you dream alone is only a dream. A dream you dream together is reality.
John Lennon

"

extensively, and to remain neutral. She avoids asking a question in a way that leads to a specific answer. She clarifies anything that confuses her— even if it means acknowledging her ignorance. Not every interchange yields insight, but to a DEO, each conversation is at least a pleasurable way to practice her social intelligence skills.

Find difference

A DEO seeks out those different from him. He wants to understand why others see or feel differently than he does. He wants to find shared values, beliefs, or behaviors that exist despite the differences. When a DEO says his company needs more female representation on its board of directors, it's not because he's pleasing the gender equality gods. He's concerned that the board underrepresents half of the human race.

DEOs need to understand differences because they want to increase their ability to communicate across gaps and beyond barriers. They know they can only do this if they put themselves into new and unfamiliar circumstances. To them, the worst place to be is in an ivory tower or any other silo of sameness.

Live in the real world

Hand in hand with seeking diversity is living in the real world. DEOs watch TV, listen to popular music, shop in local stores, try new products, sample exotic dishes, read gossip magazines, and people watch incessantly. They are fascinated by all elements of popular culture and realize the value of keeping up with it.

In addition to exposing them to novel perspectives, DEOs' awareness of everyday life helps them more readily connect to others. When a group of employees is laughing about a new viral video, they don't hush when the DEO walks by. Instead they ask if she's seen it.

Network extensively

DEOs embrace social networks. While they may have assistance in posting or tweeting, they don't shy away from the public exposure of these online forums and digital cocktail parties. They recognize them as broadcast tools, and more importantly, as a means of connecting well beyond their physical limitations. Increasingly, DEOs encourage the use of social networks as business tools, working their connective magic both inside and outside the company.

It's a rare DEO who will bemoan the loss of privacy or fears of bad publicity related to the expansion of social networks. Five years ago, no company could envision connecting to one billion people through a single medium. Thanks to Facebook, YouTube, Yahoo!, Baidu, LinkedIn, and other platforms, this is not only possible, but likely.

1 Goleman, Daniel, Richard Boyatzis, and Annie McKee. 2002. *Primal Leadership: Realizing the Power of Emotional Intelligence.* Boston: Harvard Business School Press.
2 Barsade, Sigal G. 2002. "The Ripple Effect: Emotional Contagion and Its Influence on Group Behavior." *Administrative Science Quarterly* 47 (4): 644–75.

Workouts to become more socially intelligent

Hang out.

Spend casual time with your colleagues or employees. Join them for lunch. Play on the company softball team. Share your favorite fictional novels. Organize a costume party on Halloween, a gift-sharing party at Christmas, or a potluck for the Super Bowl. If socializing with a large group is difficult for you, start with one or two colleagues and build from there.

Listen better.

Connecting with others depends on understanding them. Try rephrasing and repeating back to someone what she says. Explain that you want to comprehend her meaning and ask her to acknowledge when you get it right. Monitor the amount of time you spend talking versus listening. Avoid dominating a conversation no matter how fascinating you think you are.

We not me.

Spend a day without use the word "I" in any conversation. It's much harder to do than it seems, but even attempting to do this will force you to focus on others more than yourself.

Make friends.

Keep track of how many people you know within your company or neighborhood. Make it a game by setting goals and rewarding yourself. Obviously if you've ever been accused of stalking, this is not the workout for you. But most will find it enjoyable and harmless.

Control yourself.

Social intelligence requires self-control. If you have trouble containing your anger, get help. If you are overly judgmental, moody, or abrasive, find a coach who specializes in these areas or seminars that deal with them and work at improving over time.

GO DEEPER
PeopleSmart: Developing Your Interpersonal Intelligence by Melvin L. Silberman
Social Intelligence: The New Science of Human Relationships by Daniel Goleman
The Power of the Herd by Linda Kohanov
The Social Animal: The Hidden Sources of Love, Character, and Achievement by David Brooks

Dilbert, the popular cartoon character created by Scott Adams, works in an environment where nothing ever gets done. He moves from meeting to meeting and from plan to plan in a company that continuously circles but never lands. Bosses are incompetent but never fired. Bureaucracy is rampant but never fixed.

DEOs don't laugh at Dilbert. To them the cartoon strip and its dysfunctional characters are a very real concern and a continual reminder of their favorite three letters: GSD—an innocent-looking acronym that's short for "get shit done." In more polite terms, DEOs make things happen.

In the normal world, no one questions the value of making progress, but in the corporate world, it sometimes seems debatable. Why else would the Clinton Global Initiative need to state that its goal is "to turn ideas into action." And why else would the price of admission to this prestigious forum be not only to innovate but also to execute?

Because he fears the stickiness of inertia, a DEO learns to balance dreaming, planning, and doing. For him, perfection exists in the right distribution of effort between these three modes. An emphasis on continual innovation and brainstorming can overshadow the need to build something. An emphasis on planning, monitoring, analyzing, and reporting can inadvertently outweigh the importance of production and shipping.

DEOs' compulsion to get involved and push for completion may be rooted in one or more neuroses, but the benefits to the company far outweigh the cost. When a company's leaders include the "ability to complete tasks on time" in the skill set required for success, it signals to everyone the importance of moving the company's product, service, or experience out of the conference room and into the world.

DEOs understand the risk of too much inventiveness or too much deliberation. While they recognize the siren song of "just one more iteration," they also know that no innovation has a chance of success until it leaves the building. At some point, every awesome world-changing idea has to face the judgment of customers or clients.

Because they prize progress, DEOs become adept at prioritizing and focusing on key tasks. They push for decisions and commitments without the benefit of perfect information. They cheer first drafts and paper prototypes. They end discussions with "What's our deadline?" They attack every project, no matter how large, with the 80-20 rule: they direct the most effort where it's likely to do the most good.

DEOs' push for progress spreads and integrates the ideal that everyone should be actively engaged and focused on completion, not passively planning, rehearsing, or iterating with no end in sight. A company-wide commitment to "get shit done" means less time wasted in meetings that have no agenda. It means a ban on brainstorming sessions with no deadlines or defined output. It means a message of 140 characters might be too long.

80% of the results

are generated by 20% of the efforts

At times, a DEO's ability to GSD also means saying "no" when an opportunity lies too far beyond an organization's core competencies. This is a tough call for DEOs, particularly when markets evolve quickly and a missed prospect can doom a company. But some opportunities have to be ignored if pursuing them takes too many resources or too much management attention without a reasonable return. Trying to get too much done can be as damaging as getting too little done.

Despite the necessary strictness of the GSD trait, DEOs' enthusiasm for action is contagious. The bug is easy to catch with a commitment to get started, demote planning, set deadlines, and reward completion.

Get started

The hardest part of any project is often the start. DEOs devise ways to reduce the pain of birth. An MVP, or minimum viable product, shapes the simplest form of an idea that can be tested. Another acronym—the SFD or "shitty first draft"—encourages colleagues to make first drafts without worrying about their initial quality. A paper prototype shows what a product might look like without spending time or money on elaborate models. A series of drawings or a storyboard maps out an online experience before writing a line of code.

"

Vision without execution is hallucination.
Thomas A. Edison

"

In some organizations, DEOs face the opposite problem. Instead of too few starts, there are too many. When this happens, a DEO simply raises the bar on what constitutes a start. Ideas that don't solve a problem or address a market rarely make the cut. Potential directions that distract from core capabilities or require too much investment get extra scrutiny.

Demote planning

DEOs have a healthy distrust of extensive, highly detailed plans and an almost knee-jerk propensity to attack them and find their weak points. They treat long-term plans as they do any boilerplate document, scanning for the "meat," searching for the lean substrate that constitutes its true meaning.

A DEO doesn't summarily dismiss all plans and planning processes, but he is leery of the time they take and the content they produce. Planning meetings balloon into all-day affairs, detailing schedules and commitments that are later ignored or forgotten. Committees become enamored of their plans and produce continual updates instead of final versions. A DEO will sit through a meeting, he may even chair a committee, but he never assumes that plans equate to action or that all actions require a plan.

Set deadlines

Most people hate deadlines. They are the solid wall into which our boundless capability crashes and dies. DEOs have a different perspective. To them, deadlines are master architects, outlining the space and time available for any project. Instead of killing a DEO's creativity, a deadline shapes and defines it. It also gives him a chance to overdeliver, something a DEO rarely tires of doing.

In close cahoots with deadlines is the to-do list. Somewhere near any DEO's desk is his to-do list, filled with scribbled tasks, some circled and some scratched off. Perhaps this list is online, but most DEOs we know prefer the tangible act of writing and crossing off the actions they complete. The list helps prioritize competing activities, clarify dependencies and connections, and organize blocks of time. Take away the list and watch the equivalent of DEO withdrawal symptoms.

Reward completion

New projects are fun to start. Possibilities abound. Ideation is free-flowing. Time seems ample. Even the middle of a project is comfortable territory. Progress can be charted and additional resources engaged. But rarely is the end of a project enjoyable. The end phase is where time evaporates, choices narrow, and tempers fray.

A DEO knows the end is tougher than the start. He's personally experienced the frustration of needing more time, more talent, or more iterations but being unable to get them. He's also realized the benefit of completion. That's why there's a sign hanging somewhere near his office that reads, "Better done than perfect." That's why he praises the closers as heartily as the initiators.

Workouts to improve your GSD ability

Make a list.

If you don't already have one, start a to-do list. Don't spend hours evaluating all the digital options—just make a list of what you want to accomplish today. At the end of the day, cross off anything that's done. If you want to award yourself a badge, that's fine.

Block time.

Designate at least one day a week "meeting free." Institute this company-wide if you have the authority. If you don't, then institute it for yourself by blocking out one day on your calendar. Use this as your "catch-up" day—a time when you plow through all the half-done or almost finished items on your to-do list.

Hack it.

Try attending a Hackathon or Startup Weekend. These events are designed to produce tangible outcomes in a very short period of time. There's no room for planning. The pace is "make - test - iterate - test - iterate - test - done."

Learn improv.

Take an improvisation class. Learning to respond to prompts and create entertaining narratives without practice or a plan boosts confidence and creativity, but more importantly, it demonstrates how quickly and easily you can get something done.

Make progress.

Choose one task you've put off doing and make a tiny initial step toward completing it. Wait a day, then move it another step forward. Continue making progress in small increments until you're close enough to sprint to the end.

GO DEEPER

The 7 Habits of Highly Effective People: Powerful Lesson in Personal Change by Stephen R. Covey
The One-Minute Manager by Kenneth Blanchard and Spencer Johnson
Getting Things Done: The Art of Stress-Free Productivity by David Allen

Ayah Bdeir

Interactive artist and engineer

Ayah Bdeir is an interactive artist and engineer with the elegance and composure of a diplomat. She is the creator and CEO of littleBits, an open source library of modules that snap together, making it easy to prototype, learn, and have fun with electronics. Bdeir's goal is to move electronics from the hands of experts to those of artists, makers, students, and designers—a vision quite worthy of a DEO.

We interviewed Bdeir in a brightly colored conversation pit at a TED conference in Long Beach, California. With crowds milling about and the next session rapidly approaching, she calmly and quickly relayed how much she's accomplished in her first thirty years and described her goals for the future.

Can you recall any early childhood experiences that shaped you?

Yes, there are multiple occasions that I can recall, but one that stands out happened when I was about eight years old. My dad was a very tech-savvy man in Beirut, where I grew up. My mom worked, so I didn't know that women were raised differently from men. My dad bought my sisters and me a Commodore 64, a dot-matrix printer, and lessons in software development.

When my dad traveled, he'd bring us 3.5" floppies as gifts. One time, he brought home software to make greeting cards. I became obsessed with this software. I played with it for hours and printed out the results on the dot-matrix printer. I made cards and "Welcome home" banners for my dad, and anything else I could get it to create.

This was an important part of my creative expression as a child. As this passion evolved, I learned to write software so I could design my own stuff. I learned to express myself through digital media and it's stayed with me.

When was the first time you remember expressing yourself creatively?

I've always been creative. In school, I was always restless, reinventing the assignments. I was always interested in construction tools, like Legos. My parents noticed this early and did a good job of developing both my left and right brain. I learned both math and design.

When did you first realize you could lead?

I've always been leading, even when there was no one to lead. I led my plush toys. At sixteen, I watched the *Pippi Longstocking* movie and got very excited about extracurricular classes. My school was very traditional and didn't offer this. So I formed a lobby to demand extracurricular classes. We got one AV class. But this gave me the idea that if something wasn't there, I could make it happen.

"

I didn't start out to create a company. I wanted to solve problems.

"

The first expression of my entrenchment in the Maker Movement happened at seventeen, when my girlfriends and I created a small Maker's Faire in Beirut. We had carnivals where people went, played games, and bought stuff, but I felt these were meaningless. I wanted to create a fair where everyone could make something. We called it L'Atelier des Enfants. We got five hundred people to attend along with sponsors. We led the courses, guiding people to make something and take it home. This was thirteen years ago, and even then I was tired of kids buying and not making.

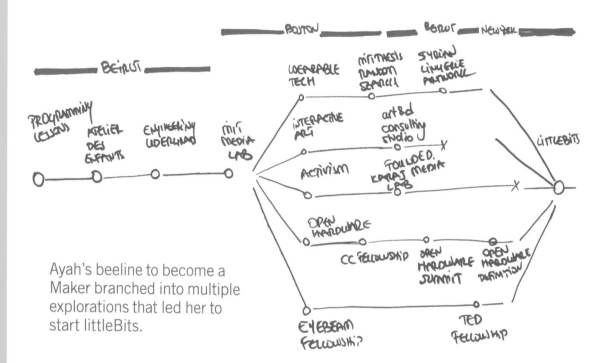

Ayah's beeline to become a Maker branched into multiple explorations that led her to start littleBits.

Have you made any course corrections yet in your career?

Lots of them—I wanted to be an architect, but my parents wanted me to be an engineer. I did what they wanted, but I hated it and spent all my time trying to think of how to make it into something I liked. I wanted to do a double major in design, but couldn't so I sat in on classes anyway. After undergrad, I applied to the MIT Media Lab for graduate school because they were beginning to support the Maker Movement.

After grad school, I moved to New York and worked in financial services. I was making good money, but one day I couldn't take it any more and I quit. I took a fellowship at EyeBeam.org (a key player in the Maker Movement) at a sharp pay cut, but teaching there was a source of energy to me.

At work, I iterate all the time. I think this is a very important trait. I'll try something and then shift if it doesn't work.

What prompted you to start your company?

I didn't start out to create a company. I wanted to solve problems. To do that I had to create products, then I needed to create a company to distribute the products.

The problems I wanted to solve? One is that developers were creating devices as one-offs even though much of the functionality was the same.

They weren't sharing the core parts with others, building on each other's work. In an extension of the open source movement, I wondered how I could make electronics modular.

Another problem was that I saw materials evolving over the past decade—cardboard, plastics, and so on. I felt that we were at a time when light, sound, and touch sensitivity needed to become creative materials.

littleBits is the result of my attempts to solve these problems. We now have twenty-two people. Our office in New York is a wonderful open space where we host workshops. We've done two successful rounds of funding: Joi Ito and Nicholas Negroponte have supplied seed funding. Our second round came from True Ventures, Khosla Ventures, and others. We offer thirty-nine products and are designing forty to fifty more.

Has your role at the company shifted over time?

Yes. Last year my biggest challenge was the amazing response to our products. I was overwhelmed just responding to the inbound. I spent most of my time just trying to keep up. My role was very reactive, solving problems as they came. I focused on tactical challenges and day-to-day issues, but also I kept experimenting. I was trying to figure out the relationship with schools and with stores, how short our product life cycle is—anything that I could experiment with.

Now I'm no longer fighting fires. I have a good team. I have a handle on my relationships. Now I'm taking a more active role in those relationships. I still have experiments going on because I think this is a complete innovation in design, technology, open source, and manufacturing. We haven't figured it out yet.

What are your strengths at work?

I'm a problem solver. I'm very good at identifying problems. I can see what is not working ahead of it actually happening. The solution to the problems often doesn't come from me, but I'm very comfortable in asking people to collaborate and getting the solutions.

My other important trait is infused in our culture. It's "no ego." The best idea wins. It doesn't matter where it comes from.

And your weaknesses?

I try to reinvent too many things. I obsess about a problem at the expense of other stuff. Last year we had a spam problem with our website. I spent an entire week trying to reprogram the website. There were more important things I could have focused on.

Can you describe your leadership style now?

Yes, my leadership style is changing as the company grows. Some pieces I'm trying to maintain and some have to change. When I first started I led by doing. I saw a cartoon where everyone was in a boat and the leader was helping everyone pull it forward, while the manager was giving instructions on how to pull. That image stuck in my mind. I felt I wouldn't be able to lead if I wasn't in the weeds with everyone else, among the details. If I wasn't doing the work, I wouldn't know what's possible and what's unreasonable.

I'm keeping some of this style, but now I lead by doing modules of the work then giving it to others so I can also focus on more long-term issues and direction. For example, I will get involved with an initiative and work with everyone as it's being developed. I'm very proud that I can take feedback and iterate. But as an initiative takes off, I move on to something else and let others take over.

How do you lead in an industry that is constantly changing?

Change is not unique to us, but certainly it's very common among technology companies. It's just our reality. To deal with it, you have to learn every day. I'm constantly asking other founders questions, talking to staff members, and reading online comments from users. I have to learn every day but I also want to learn—I find it fun.

If people are resistant to change or can't deal with it, they don't stay with us long. Whether they make the decision or we do, they leave. We surround ourselves with people who can change easily. Sometimes there's a downside to this. Sometimes we think too much about changes. Like when we choose new software—is this the best calendaring software or is this new version better? Sometimes I just have to say, "This is not perfect, but we're going with it."

Do you think innovation depends more on process or people?

Our approach has definitely come from my engineering training. The process is basically have an idea, test it, iterate. We're all constantly inspired by everything around us. Whether I'm at an art gallery or a hardware store or watching Top Chef, I'll see something that inspires me and I'll email it to everyone. We all do this, so I'd say our innovation is a combination of people and process. We inspire each other and iterate.

> "
> # The best idea wins. It doesn't matter where it comes from.
> "

What do you love most about your job?

I love going to events, demos, and workshops and seeing people use littleBits. I love seeing their faces light up—whether they're big or small, the reaction is the same. First there's this moment of wonder, followed by this moment of empowerment or comprehension. I love seeing this happen. If I'm having an off day, it just picks me right up. When I don't have events to attend, I search YouTube for videos from users who want to show what they've created.

Is corporate culture important to you?

One of the best pieces of advice I got when I started my company was to hire for cultural fit before skills. I'll choose someone with cultural fit and the ability to acquire the right skills over someone who's overqualified but isn't a good cultural fit. If we don't get the cultural fit right, it causes all kinds of problems—resentment, ego battles, gossip. Ego just can't exist at littleBits.

We're a culture of people driven by a passion for our mission and for what we do. Because we're driven by our passion to help others be creative, we accept that a solution can come from anyone—it can come from me or an intern or from user feedback. It doesn't matter. We only care about finding the best solution to the problem. We're also not about punching a clock or strict schedules. We're about accountability. As long as you get the work done, we don't care how long you work.

Do you control or influence your corporate culture?

Some parts of it I control, for instance, the no ego thing. I'll intervene if I think someone is gossiping or letting their ego get in the way. I'll tell them directly, "This is not what we do here." But our mission also attracts people who are passionate about what we do. They don't join us for the money or the perks. They join us because they want to spread tools of creativity, enrich the lives of children, and help make the world better—not because of our 401(k) program or vacation policy.

Is the space where you work important to you?

Our space is very important. In fact, it was a very deliberate decision and I spent an inordinate amount of time looking for it. I knew we couldn't move into just any space. We had to stay in Manhattan and below 14th Street. This is the creative heart of New York. It has the right cachet to attract a certain type of person—different from who we'd attract if we were in Brooklyn.

Also, we chose a loft building with high ceilings and open spaces in a charming, six-story building. We don't even have a building manager. In it, we created common spaces. We have a studio with electronics and machines. We have a play space—not a pretend one, but a place where we

A child plays with littleBits in the company's open space.

want people to play. We have toys everywhere and it's colorful. It's a very unique space and you experience it the minute you walk in.

When you're gone from the scene, what three things do you want to be known for?

One, I'd like to be known as a problem solver. Two, that I helped bring other people's creativity to life—people who maybe didn't think they had it in them to make creative things. Three, that I was ambitious.

CO-CREATION

partnership builds relationship

smaller teams rock

respect expertise

seek diverse opinions

clarify roles & responsibilities

seek shared values

go wide

NETWORKS & CONNECTIONS

seek experts

be open

recognize contribution

allow information to travel

encourage serendipity

learn continuously

attend events outside your industry

CARE & FEEDING

valued employees become more productive & loyal

understand what people value

fellowship = sense of belonging

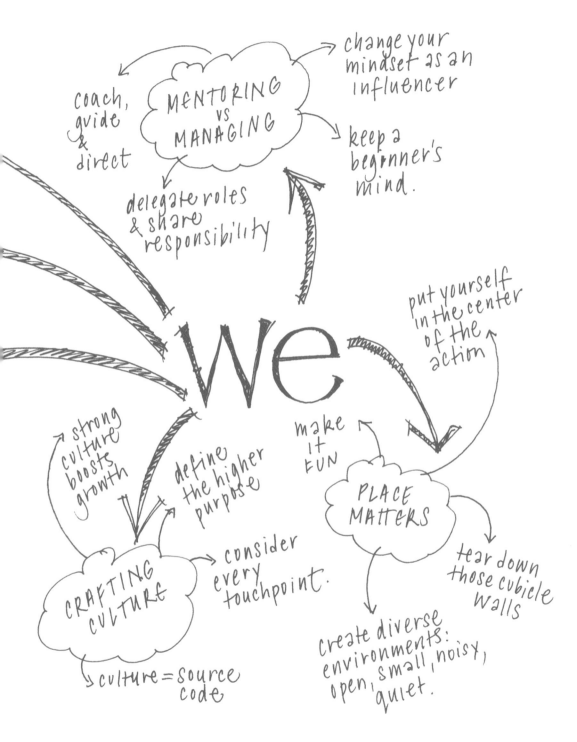

change your mindset as an influencer

keep a beginner's mind.

coach, guide & direct

MENTORING vs MANAGING

delegate roles & share responsibility

put yourself in the center of the action

we

strong culture boosts growth

define the higher purpose

make it FUN

PLACE MATTERS

tear down those cubicle walls

consider every touchpoint.

CRAFTING CULTURE

culture = source code

create diverse environments: open, small, noisy, quiet.

CO-CREATION

We've evolved into a society where few can create value alone. Producing a simple ebook reader requires the cooperation of thousands of people across multiple continents. DEOs find this energizing. They are happy to join the co-creative crowd.

A team co-created this book. Maria framed the initial concept and Christopher collaborated on writing and content, but on our own we couldn't have completed it. A colleague helped find relevant research studies for us. The profiled DEOs shared their experience and advice.

Designers improved the book's engagement and readability. A copy editor corrected grammar and improved clarity. Others provided marketing, printing, and legal support. Although only the authors are visibly associated with the title, this book would not exist without our co-creative partners.

This book is a relatively simple product. When we consider more malleable experiences, like social networks and digital environments, co-creation extends beyond initial conception or production and becomes a permanent relationship. Teams of coders, user-experience designers, developers, search engine optimization specialists, legal experts, researchers, and users all collaborate and co-create daily. Their efforts generate the product's content, and as a result, much of its value.

Some have described co-creation as a response to greater complexity or the need for greater efficiency. These definitions fit, but co-creation and the collaboration that it enables provide DEOs with a few notable superpowers.

We can be more insightful and more intelligent collectively than we can individually.[1] Even creativity is boosted through collective effort, provided the group is diverse. A fascinating study by Brian Uzzi and Jarrett Spiro analyzed the impact of collaboration on the artistic and financial success of Broadway plays. Perhaps counterintuitively, creative success was more likely if the production mixed experienced and novice participants. Newer members brought fresh ideas and novel interpretations. Experienced collaborators helped integrate innovations to make them more accessible and popular.

When co-creation includes extending help to colleagues, as is common with collaborative teams, a company's bottom line can benefit as well. In studying the effectiveness of government intelligence teams, Harvard researchers found that the strongest predictor of group effectiveness was the amount of help that analysts gave to each other.[2]

Because a DEO recognizes the beneficial effect of "we," she is adept at encouraging and promoting collaboration, cooperation, and teamwork. She routinely acknowledges and rewards it in public and in private. She admires the creative twist contributed by a graphic designer. She notices when a purchasing agent improves a product's quality through creative sourcing. She acknowledges an accountant's insights into how to provide customers with more value. She thanks the delivery person for contributing to the team's efficiency.

Collaboration is the number one trait corporate leaders most desire in employees.

IBM Leading Through Connections. 2012.

This acknowledgement sends the message that collaborators are valued and respected. They are not just staff workers hired to do rote jobs. They are partners in the design process, and their skills and experience directly impact the quality and appeal of the company's product, service, or experience.

A DEO will integrate more stakeholders into the creative process, increasing everyone's feelings of inclusion and commitment. She extends this collaborative web beyond the office by treating clients and vendors as co-creators, respecting the expertise and experience they bring. Vendors who participate in defining a problem can provide better options. Clients who help create a solution are more likely to adopt it.

Given the clear benefits of co-creation, it's no surprise that DEOs find ways to make it flourish in their organizations by encouraging greater agility, diversity, and clarity.

Go agile
Co-creation may seem unwieldy and chaotic, but if managed well, it can be more efficient and responsive than a siloed or phase-driven process. The "agile" development system used extensively by software engineers is a model of collaborative proficiency.

With this method, solutions form incrementally as teams work across functional areas, iterating and building together. This focus on smaller, interrelated parts helps the development team respond to rapidly changing business needs without starting over. It supports pivots or revisions necessitated by new information or changed market conditions. Teams develop a greater sense of each other's contributions and a heightened sensitivity to interdependencies.

Seek diversity

To get the most out of collaboration and co-creation, a DEO demands diversity in teams, not only in ethnicity or gender, but also in age, expertise, and even interests or hobbies. She encourages senior leaders to consider the viewpoints of junior members, while similarly encouraging young professionals to listen carefully to the advice of people with lengthy careers.

Even different cognitive types matter. A study of research and development teams found that innovation is improved if the collaboration balances "creatives" with those who are "detail-oriented" and "conformists."[3] A DEO urges musicians to influence accountants, engineers to inspire artists, and gatekeepers to align with rebels.

Clarify roles

A DEO recognizes that successful collaboration depends on well-defined roles and clear communication. The right information needs to be delivered to the right people in the right way at the right time and in the right place.

A simple heuristic that adds clarity is to define three types of participants in each group: an owner, influencers, and participants. The owner is responsible for the group's overall success and is the final decision maker. Influencers

Co-creation's optimal balance of cognitive types:

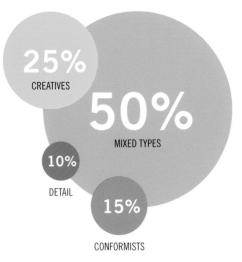

Miron-Spektor, Ella, Erez, Miriam and Naveh, Eitan. "To Drive Creativity, Add Some Conformity." *Harvard Business Review.*

add expertise, critiques, feedback, and opinions. Participants contribute their talents to the actual design and development of the project.

This clarity of roles and responsibilities counters the tendency for collaborations to suffer from the quaintly phrased dysfunction: "too many chiefs and not enough Indians." It also allows the DEO to choose her role in a collaboration and to avoid always being the owner.

1 Surowiecki, James. 2004. *The Wisdom of Crowds.* New York: Doubleday.
2 Grant, Adam. 2013. "Givers Take All: The Hidden Dimension of Corporate Culture." *McKinsey Quarterly.*
3 Miron-Spektor, Ella, Miriam Erez, and Eitan Naveh. March 2012. "To Drive Creativity, Add Some Conformity." *Harvard Business Review.* http://hbr.org/2012/03/to-drive-creativity-add-some-conformity/ar/1

Workouts to make you a better co-creator

Keep silent.

If you suspect that others depend too much on your initiative, try faking laryngitis in your next planning meeting. Limit your responses to nods and smiles. No matter what happens in the meeting, keep silent and encourage those around you to pick up the slack. Once the group understands that moving forward is up to them and that you support them, they'll engage more.

Give it up.

If you're a designer, try giving up ownership of that term. Share it with anyone who contributes to a solution or new concept. Make it a descriptor of an activity rather than a person or position. Think of design as an active verb, not an overused and passive noun.

Welcome strangers.

For your next brainstorming session, seek out as diverse a group as you can find and watch what happens. Never included the janitor, receptionist, or accounts receivable clerk? Try it and see what happens. Don't stop with the obvious choices. Seek diversity that isn't obvious. Learn about people's hobbies or nonbusiness interests. Stamp collectors, drone builders, quilters, and amateur archeologists might not seem relevant to your project, until they contribute the most important insight.

Run credits.

In your next presentation, take a cue from Hollywood and include a slide that credits everyone who contributed to your talk. Extend the thank-yous by posting them on Facebook or broadcasting them on Twitter.

GO DEEPER
Wikinomics: How Mass Collaboration Changes Everything by Donald Tapscott and Anthony D. Williams
The Wealth of Networks: How Social Production Transforms Markets and Freedom by Yochai Benkler
Group Genius: The Creative Power of Collaboration by Keith Sawyer
Crowdsourcing: Why the Power of the Crowd Is Driving the Future of Business by Jeff Howe
Redesigning Leadership by John Maeda and Rebecca J. Bermont

A DEO swims in a sea of interrelated employees, partners, shareholders, influencers, customers, and commenters. Far from imagining himself as "King of the Hill," a DEO knows that his role is to connect and maintain healthy relationships.

Strong, effective networks are not only a sign of a DEO's social competence, but also a way he creates value. Traditionally a leader's network evolved from his college classmates. It grew linearly through work relationships and eventually industry associations. The goal, stated or implied, was to connect with the most influential people, using other connections as stepping-stones to the top levels. Networking was the process of finding and following those stepping-stones by dispensing an ever-flowing supply of business cards and a hearty handshake.

Undoubtedly some people continue to use networks in this limited way, but they're not DEOs. A DEO sees a much broader benefit to networking and incorporates myriad ways of building, using, and maintaining them outside his company and inside.

Networks and communities, whether online or in person, feed a DEO information and shape his perspective. Through his network he can scan gigabits of data, form ideas on the fly, and fill knowledge gaps quickly. When he in turn contributes information to his network, it raises his visibility and promotes his company. The network supplies an audience for his pitch or presentation by connecting him to equally experienced professionals ready to praise or critique.

A DEO's network can also reveal opportunities: it can identify new clients or customers, find viable candidates, and link to potential investors. If it's built on one or more social networks, it can magnify the DEO's reach well beyond the conferences, trade shows, and conventions he can attend in person. Ideally, a DEO's network even connects him with his customers. If his customers number in the millions, perhaps this connection is not a true dialogue, but it's sufficient to give customers a sense of the DEO's character and beliefs.

DEOs strive to construct two types of networks: deep ones composed of experts and specialists, and wide ones uniting a broad range of people who may have little in common. Each network delivers different value to the DEO.

To build a deep network, a DEO looks for and links to professionals and experts with a shared focus. If the DEO is in a field with well-developed specialties, he may just need to link to existing deep networks. Professional associations whose members share similar skill sets like the AIGA (American Institute of Graphic Arts) or the PGA (Professional Golfers' Association of America) are examples of narrowly focused but deep networks.

If a DEO is exploring a topic that doesn't have an existing professional association or similar community, he can easily start one thanks to the proliferation of social networks and online forums designed to connect the like-minded. Expert networks form daily on LinkedIn and Facebook in the guise of groups. They can emerge ad hoc on Twitter when united by a specific hashtag like #DesignResearch or #RiseoftheDEO.

Over the next five years, CEO participation in social media will grow from its current level of 16% to 57%.

IBM Leadership Through Connections. 2012.

When a DEO joins or starts a deep network, he is typically seeking more detailed information than is publicly available. He may hope to learn from others' mistakes or benefit from others' explorations. He may wish to compare experiences or confirm suspicions. He may be seeking a shortcut to prequalified talent, clients, or contractors. Paul Graham, founder of Y Combinator, a hugely successful Silicon Valley startup accelerator, created Hacker News as a way for his community of technology startups to share and rate information. He encourages entrepreneurs to post and comment as a means of introducing themselves, their capabilities, and their attitudes; in essence, he uses this deep network to screen candidates for his accelerator.

DEOs also build wide networks that include "weak links" to other communities. In this case, a weak link is someone the DEO knows but who is outside his normal circle of friends or colleagues. By including links to the people a DEO doesn't know well, or doesn't interact with often, he connects to other networks and, as a result, to a much larger and more diverse population. Weak links allow information to travel from one network to the next, greatly expanding its potential to spread. This benefits the DEO by giving him greater reach, and increases his creative potential by giving him access to less homogenous information. A DEO connected to a large and wide network gains more exposure to new ideas, data, and perspectives.

These wider networks of loosely connected people also make it theoretically possible to link to anyone. Studies have consistently proved that we're all separated by no more than six links (or degrees) from each other. Rather than networking crazily in hopes of connecting to the right person, a DEO who uses an online networking service can see his network and can easily find the best path to a new contact—no matter who it is. Yes, that's correct. The Six Degrees of Kevin Bacon game is based on real science. DEOs take it seriously.

Networks and communities are so valuable that DEOs usually take personal responsibility for identifying, building, and maintaining them. Like ood friends, the connections that make up a network require care and feeding. A DEO curates his social and business networks by looking for shared values, respecting virality and encouraging serendipity.

Seek shared value

Since connections and communities can influence perspectives and shape information access, DEOs avoid networks with values in conflict with their own. Some networks are so large that they're value-neutral, but most have an aim or goal of their own. DEOs carefully assess the composition and intent of a network by checking its members' profiles, reviewing its posted content, and checking out its sponsors. If the network gathers at regular meetups or other events, the DEO will attend and talk to its members to determine whether the group fits with his existing network.

The public visibility of a DEO's network connections is generally positive, but it does make him vulnerable to the old adage "you are judged by the company you keep."

Respect virality

The same interdependencies that speed information sharing, raise visibility, and identify new opportunities can become potent and almost unstoppable sources of disruption. Networks don't necessarily screen out falsehoods, poor data, or bad actors. Similarly, they spread news of a failure just as efficiently as they do that of a success. As several high-profile people recently learned, networks are terrible at keeping secrets.

A DEO acknowledges and respects the two-way flow of a network and its inability to conform to a company's marketing plans. He learns to disregard the ignorant post and the incessant spam. He hopes that being open and honest will be rewarded. He knows that trying to hide anything significant from a connected world is the fastest way to be lambasted on *The Daily Show* or *The Colbert Report*.

Encourage serendipity

The "happy accident" of serendipity can be bred out of networks if they're too closed, too narrowly conceived, or ironically, too wide. A steady flow of serendipitous discoveries, whether of people, information, or potential, is a good indicator that a network is the right size and composition. If it's not generating anything surprisingly useful on a regular basis, then some pruning or planting is in order.

One way DEOs add to the diversity and potential of their networks is by regularly attending events outside their industry. TED conferences are infamous for mixing auto execs with geologists and mathematicians with clothing designers, accelerating the possibility of serendipitous magic. There are a host of other events that provide a similar benefit. To DEOs, these gatherings are the perfect mashup of novel ideas and new connections—in other words, the building blocks of their networks.

Workouts to increase your connectivity

Join in.

If you haven't already joined an online social network, do it now. Start with a basic one like LinkedIn and build up to more advanced ones like Google+ or Facebook. If you're intimidated by posting, simply lurk for a while until you have something to say. If you'd rather communicate through photos or videos, try Instagram or YouTube.

Say hi.

If you're attending a conference, set a goal for how many new people you'll meet. Introduce yourself to whoever sits next to you in the auditorium or stands next to you in line for coffee. Find an interest or perspective you share and exchange contact information if that seems worthwhile. Don't make the mistake of working the room, moving quickly from one superficial conversation to the next. It's obvious and unbecoming.

Reach out.

The next time you're sharing insights or valued information, deliberately reach out to people who are different from your normal circle of friends or colleagues. Consider including people like your insurance agent, your neighbor, or your son-in-law's parents in your distribution. They might ignore your share, or they might pass it along to your next client.

Share more.

Develop the habit of sharing regularly. The content can be minimal, but it should be meaningful. There's no shortage of jokes circulating through email, and we have a full quota of cat videos.

GO DEEPER

Connected by Nicholas A. Christakis and James H. Fowler
Sync: How Order Emerges From Chaos In the Universe, Nature, and Daily Life by Steven H. Strogatz
Linked by Albert-László Barabási
Lives by Nicholas A. Christakis and James H. Fowler
Business, Science, and Everyday Life by Albert-László Barabási

MENTORING VS. MANAGING

DEOs don't manage, they mentor. Managing is about control, conformity, monitoring, and standards. Mentoring is about growth and guidance, about helping people become proficient, and cheering them to exceed any standard. In short, mentoring moves a company forward, while managing holds it in place.

Mentoring benefits not only the employee, but also the company and the DEO. Clearly the employee gets valuable training and career development, but mentoring also can have a substantial effect on job and career satisfaction. Greater job and career satisfaction increases productivity, raises morale, and improves retention.[1]

If those sizable benefits aren't convincing enough, consider the employment expectations of Millennials. The 80 million or more people who make up this young cohort in the United States are entering the workplace in droves, queuing up to replace retiring baby boomers. Among the many traits they share are a desire for fulfillment in their jobs and a preference for continual feedback. They look to company leaders for career development and mentoring.

A traditional CEO might complain about Millennials suffering from a sense of entitlement or being overly narcissistic. A DEO sees an opportunity to attract and keep the best young talent.

Rather than being burdened by the responsibility of mentoring, a DEO finds it personally rewarding. It's an efficient means of knowledge sharing, particularly since younger workers bring their own valuable information to share. Mentoring provides useful training to a 25-year-old employee. In exchange, the younger worker can show his mentor how to use Twitter for gathering news or Instagram for communicating through photos.

A DEO also sees mentoring as an easy and accurate way to retain the sense of what it's like to be a novice. This connection helps him keep in touch with parts of the company that may not always reach his desk. It gives him a chance to see his business through a "beginner's mind," bringing the gift of openness, enthusiasm, and lack of preconceptions to a topic that may have grown stale for the DEO.

DEOs have numerous and customized approaches to mentoring. No one way is favored. Traditional career development mentoring works for some. A DEO will counsel, guide, and direct an employee through various stages of his career, continually providing him with appropriate challenges and opportunities.

Apprenticeships are another form of mentoring, in which an employee observes, follows, and emulates someone more experienced. Some DEOs prefer a simple knowledge transfer, explaining and teaching what they know to others either in formal settings like colleges or conferences, or ad hoc in the lunchroom or hallway. In some cases, DEOs become coaches, inspiring and pushing a team of protégés toward a desired goal.

Change your mindset

More important than the approach is the mindset change that is required to replace managing with mentoring. Managing is focused on the manager and the result of his actions. Mentoring is focused on the employee and the gains he achieves. Carl Bass, CEO of Autodesk, compares mentoring to parenting:

"I think it's a lot like being a parent: you learn to pass on knowledge and skills. They'll take what they want from me and get rid of much of it. But, you know, it's a way of influencing."

Management identifies behaviors and attitudes and seeks to strengthen or reform them. Mentoring looks at the whole person and seeks to help him grow within the company or find something more suitable. It doesn't ignore outside activities. Instead it integrates them.

The top five characteristics Millennials want in a boss:

1. Will help me navigate my career path

2. Will give me straight feedback

3. Will mentor and coach me

4. Sponsor me for formal development programs

5. Is comfortable with flexible schedules

Meister, Jeanne C. and Willyerd, Karie. May 2010. "Mentoring Millennials." Harvard Business Review. http://hbr.org/2010/05/mentoring-Millennials/ar/1

Mentor	Manager
Supports and guides personal growth	Monitors and assesses performance
Offers advice as needed and appropriate	Provides limited feedback on specific criteria
Two-way dialog	Top-down communication
Interested in long-term career development	Interested in short-term task completion
Not necessarily a direct reporting relationship	Direct reporting relationship
Opens doors and makes introductions	Not typically interested in furthering career goals
Can become a friend	Less likely to become a friend
Champions risk taking and new challenges	Often discourages risk taking

If an employee is constantly distracted and unproductive at work, a manager might fire him. A mentor might discover that the employee is learning to code in his spare time and encourage him to apply for a position that matches his interest more directly.

Delegate roles

Mentoring doesn't eliminate delegation; it just remodels it. Instead of piecing out responsibilities and delegating the menial or less rewarding tasks to subordinates as a manager might do, a DEO delegates his entire role. He assumes everyone can become a DEO and mentors them to act as one, even in the most limited circumstances. He knows that a company full of DEOs-in-training will mostly manage itself.

A DEO may not be able to avoid all management responsibilities, but he can create systems or structures that reduce the need for them. For example, Zappos cofounder and CEO Tony Hsieh will pay any new hire $1,000 to quit. He does this to quickly eliminate anyone who doesn't really want to work at the company, effectively identifying and reversing a "bad hire" before someone else needs to manage the problem.

This shift in focus from the manager to the person being mentored is crucial for success. A DEO tries to role model this new perspective and instill it in every stakeholder.

1 Grant, Adam. 2013. "Givers Take All: The Hidden Dimension of Corporate Culture." *McKinsey Quarterly,* April. http://www.mckinsey.com/insights/organization/givers_take_all_the_hidden_dimension_of_corporate_culture; and Harvard Business School Press. 2004. *Coaching and Mentoring: How to Develop Top Talent and Achieve Stronger Performance.* Boston: Harvard Business School.

Workouts to improve your mentoring

Start young.

If you're not yet comfortable with mentoring, start outside your company by teaching young people. Coach a kids' sports team, volunteer for Big Brothers or Big Sisters, or host a Girl Scout or Boy Scout troop. Teach a child how to do an art project, play music, build a fort, or spell. The list is endless and it's all a form of mentoring.

Trade tips.

Once you gain confidence in your role, graduate to adults. Create an informal mentoring exchange agreement with a friend—you help me accomplish X, I'll help you with Y. If you need a little more distance and time to prepare, volunteer to mentor online.

Meet up.

If you're personally comfortable mentoring and want to see your company embrace it more fully, try creating an informal mentoring meetup. Convince a more experienced or senior person to be the mentor and invite others who want to learn or grow in a specific area.

Take two.

Encourage your company to build mentoring into orientation. Pair more senior team members with new employees for a set period of time, not only to help them navigate the office and its politics, but also to share perspectives in both directions.

Trade places.

Try being mentored to learn what works and what doesn't. Ask someone younger to mentor you on using social networks or your iPhone. Ask someone of the opposite gender to mentor you on communicating more effectively. Pay attention to when and how you learn best and incorporate those techniques into your own mentoring.

GO DEEPER

A Game Plan for Life: The Power of Mentoring by John Wooden and Don Yaeger
Monday Morning Leadership: 8 Mentoring Sessions You Can't Afford to Miss by David Cottrell
Mentoring: The Tao of Giving and Receiving Wisdom by Chungliang Al Huang and Jerry Lynch

Jesse Ziff Cool

Entrepreneur and author

Jesse smiles as though she's shy. At heart, she may be, but in practice she's an extroverted DEO who has greeted and fed thousands of customers, including Oprah Winfrey, Steve Jobs, and Bill Gates. The creative force behind five unique restaurants and seven cookbooks, she's dedicated herself to sustainable agriculture and cuisine for over thirty-five years.

We interviewed Cool at her home in Palo Alto, California, after a tour of her vegetable garden, fruit trees, and chicken coop. Sitting in her large and highly functional yet comfortable kitchen, she explained how her career and her life grew out of her passion for good food.

Did any early experiences influence who you are today?

My father was in the grocery business and I had an uncle who was a butcher. Growing up in a Jewish-Italian family means food was everywhere. As a little girl, I'd go to the refrigerator and make lists of ingredients. Then I'd take those lists to my family and ask what they wanted to eat. My brothers loved it. I'd drag out tables and chairs and make little restaurants outside for everyone. I'd make places for them to sit and eat. There's so much love and connection that comes from food. When you feed people, you can feel that connection. It's nurturing.

Do you think of yourself as creative?

Yes, my medium is food. Whenever I've needed to take care of myself, my inspiration has always been through food. With it, I've created deliciousness and political connection with the environment, and connection with my staff.

I feel creative on many levels. I think of gardening as creative. I connect to my plants, the dirt, my chickens. I also love to cook. My happiest moments are cranking up the music, having something to drink, and cooking for hours.

How do you recognize creativity in others?

I look to see if they have a connection to whatever drives their passion first. If someone is a potter, he should be able to feel the clay. If someone is sensual—if they use sight, hearing, taste, feeling to connect—they'll find a way to be creative through that connection. It will bring forth an idea, a manifestation of beauty or something deliciously wonderful.

For cooking, it's similar. I look to see if they understand the ingredients. If they have a sensual connection with the ingredients, then creativity will bound and grow from that connection. Of course they have to have skills—they have to understand how to use salt, sugar, fats, acids, the basic palette. An artistic appreciation and connection flows beyond that understanding.

When I see that someone has a real sensitivity to subtle flavors and doesn't try to trick the eater with flavors, that's a good sign. I look for someone who connects to the source of the food, who starts with ingredients—how they're grown, treated, nurtured, loved. A creative cook will start with a connection to the basic ingredient and then add the right things or do the right things to enhance it.

Do you think of yourself as a good businessperson?

No, I struggled to learn how to be in business. What I know about business came from the old-fashioned ethic of working hard and serving the community, but I didn't really understand how to run a business. At my first restaurant, Late for the Train, I did everything. I hand-printed every menu, I went to the market, and I cooked the food. I didn't really think of it as a business. It was more a natural exchange of services.

Jesse hitches a ride to California and begins a career steeped in cooking, creativity, and cultural change.

But I've always been really good at counting things. I was taught to have integrity, so I thought of myself as a "waste manager." I intuitively kept costs down because I found waste disgraceful. I think that's what kept me afloat when I didn't know anything about business.

When the economy fell apart in the early 2000s, I was maxed out on everything. An advisor said I should declare bankruptcy, but I couldn't imagine not paying people back. Instead I started working with advisors and learned the really difficult foreign language called Quick-Books. My advisor taught me to hire people who are different from me. I learned how to be a woman in the business world; instead of giving everything away, I could save money and reach my goal. Now I get it.

Have you made any course corrections in your career?

Most of the time I had no clue what I was going to do next. I just kept doing what seemed right. One day I was sitting with a friend and he introduced me, saying, "Here's Jesse. She's an author." I said, "I'm not author! I'm a restaurant owner." That was an epiphany. I thought I'd been going around trying to run my business and get publicity, and as part of that I'd written four books.

JONAH & JOSHUA TRAVELED THE PATH — SO THEY WAITED THEY COULD THERE ME TO FOR NEW MOM (NOT ANY MORE)

JONAH / JOSHUA

MY 4 MEN

LEARNED TO DO BUSINESS

ALMOS BANKRUPT

THE YOUNG CONNECTED FOOD TO EVERYTHING & CHANGED EVERYTHING

7 COOK BOOKS
MERCURY NEWS
FITNESS MAGAZINE
(AM I A WRITER TOO!)

BACK TO COOKING AT HOME & FAMILY

BACK TO FOOD, FAMILY & COMMUNITY

SUPPORTING NEW PIONEERS OR FARMING & FOOD

FAMILY FRIENDS

The epiphany was realizing that I was a restaurant owner and also had become a writer!

Did you overcome any hurdles in building your business?

I've been near bankruptcy more times than I'd like to admit. But I was always willing to go out the door and quit rather than not use organic, local produce. So I knew I cared about that principle and I would not change it. I had to learn to design the business around that core

"

If I take good care of my staff, then they'll take good care of everything else.

"

belief. Fortunately, the world changed. Now people agree that there should be a connection between food and local growers, so the business is prospering.

I'm not a feminist, but women traditionally didn't belong in the food industry. This made me stronger and tougher. Women in food can't have a period. They can't talk. Can't cry. Can't complain. This challenge taught me how to build a business structure that's also good for people. Our community taught me about the value of longevity. They trust me. I get so much help from everyone. I'm so particular that I used to want to do it all myself. It was really hard to learn to let go of some things.

What's your leadership style now?

My philosophy at work is "the customer comes last." By that I mean that if I take good care of my staff, then they'll take good care of everything else. So I manage from the bottom up. I'm a support for others to get things done. But I also have really high standards. I'm particular and detailed, which some describe as "picky bitch." I work hard so I expect everyone to work hard. I hope that

everyone collaborates, shares ideas, and helps each other to collectively create change. It is also important to balance the old and the new. There is a lovely connection in balancing tradition and innovation that can bring stability and newness.

Is corporate culture important to your business?

On a scale of 1 to 10, it's a 10. People work hard. They should feel proud of their work. I want them to feel that they're in the best place they could be. They eat better, they get the best money, and they're given responsibility for their team. I have a core philosophy based on the connection of food to the farm—my coworkers have to be able to tell this story. I want them to be themselves and yet a part of our story as long as possible, so we all keep evolving and changing.

We live in a privileged community and sometimes this intrudes on our values, but we try to ignore it. We're really doing well right now and it's easy to get the wrong attitude. I keep reminding everyone that we're here to serve and care for people. Some people ask a lot, but we remind our staff that their job is to care for people.

Do you create this culture or does it just happen?

Both. We do things to attract the best talent. For instance, the primary reason I grew my business was so I could get better benefits for my employees. Because of our employee policy, we attract people who may not have experience, but we can usually help them learn to care for clients. If they can't—if they're needy themselves or just want to be nurtured without passing it on—then we bounce them out really fast. If they think they're going to be taken care of, without giving to the community, they're gone.

Though we have natural turnover in our business, the culture is much more family-like. We have had people working with us for a very long time … 5, 10, even 18 years! It means that I am a part of it all, but they actually are just as important to the company culture. I believe they know they are a part of our identity.

When did you first realize you could lead others?

In fourth grade, my mother got called in to the school and they told her I was bossy. I wanted to be the teacher. I'd rather rename bossy to "can direct." I saw things in a way others didn't and I wanted to manage people. I wanted things to be different. I didn't fit in until I moved to California.

How do you deal with risk?

I'm a radical conservative. I'm calculating about the risks I take. I was taught as a child to go as far as you can toward danger, but when you see danger, you stop. I do that. I jump into new ventures and figure out how it works later. I take something on because of an idea … to change and create something new and exciting for me and the businesses. Most often, it starts with a location that is cool or has a reasonable lease. Then I think about the food or a menu before any thought of viability.

I am not afraid to risk. At this point, after so many starts that needed major adjustments, I know that when something doesn't work, we'll just keep changing until we find ways to make it work. For some that is risky. For me and my staff, that is just being realistic.

My employees trust me. They trust that together we will figure things out because we always do. I have often said that the best lessons are from watching someone else's challenges or mistakes

Jesse visits her backyard chicken coop, a place where poultry and sculpture live in harmony.

and how they fixed them. We all learn this way. That internal business risk, though it might seem costly, is far less costly than not taking any risk at all.

When you're gone from the scene, what three things do you want to be known for?

One, for truly living the full cycle of sustainability in all aspects of my life and business. Two, for being a lot of fun, for being up for play and adventure at any age. And three, for being both soft and strong: that my children knew they were so loved and that I lived a meaningful, fabulous adventure full of martinis, great food, and a love of life.

CRAFTING CULTURE

Some believe company culture can be mandated from the top down. Some believe it emerges on its own from the bottom up. A DEO sidesteps this debate. She knows it must be built—iteratively, collaboratively, and over time—from the inside out.

Culture is the unique collection of beliefs and practices that communicates a company's values, whether or not they've been formalized or articulated. A well-designed culture unites stakeholders in a shared understanding of "the right thing to do." It becomes the unseen but firmly rooted infrastructure that coaches new hires and comforts old-timers. It's the force that attracts like-minded talent and repels those with different attitudes or behaviors. A positive company culture can boost growth, while a negative or mediocre one can speed failure.

A DEO recognizes the power of company culture, but that's not the primary reason she embraces and builds it. For a DEO, crafting an effective, authentic, and meaningful company culture is neither a choice nor a checklist item. It's a straightforward reflection of who she is and why she wants to lead. A strong company culture reflects the DEO's own beliefs and behavior.

Culture is highly subjective in its origin and evolutionary development; no template exists. In fact, copied or commanded culture is inherently dysfunctional. A culture must emerge from and accurately embody a company's people and processes. There is, however, a progression that DEOs initiate.

Purpose

Ask a DEO to build her ideal company culture, and she'll almost always start with its purpose. She'll want to make it clear not only what the company does, but also what higher commitment it serves. If this purpose is captured in a mission statement it won't be a bland functional promise like "Lead in customer satisfaction, product quality, and employee happiness," but rather a more daring, sincere, and consequential statement like that from shoe and eyewear maker, TOMS:

"With every product you purchase, TOMS will help a person in need. One for One.®"

This mission doesn't spell out exactly how the company's culture operates, but it certainly provides distinct guidance and a clear ethic for making creative or business decisions. It's scaffolding on which the company can layer additional operations, marketing, sales, or financial directives. It's source code that can be carefully edited as the company grows and changes.

Pace and Drive

In shaping company culture, a DEO strives to support creativity and curiosity. She wants a philosophy that encourages collaboration and rewards useful risk-taking, not as attributes of selected people or departments but as characteristics of the entire company. She knows these attributes need to be baked into the culture from the top down and from the bottom up. She knows these attributes thrive in an environment that feels open, approachable, transparent, and genuine.

A DEO can't completely control every detail of a healthy company culture, but she'll set the company in motion, determining whether

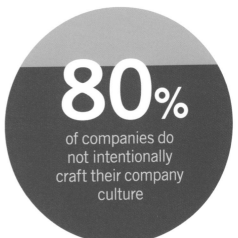

80%

of companies do not intentionally craft their company culture

Atkinson, Philip E. 1990. Creating Cultural Change: The Key to Successful Total Quality Management.

development is "fast and furious" or "slow and steady." She'll bolster admired activities and work to eliminate undesired ones. She'll model how she expects others to deal with deadlines, stress, and setbacks.

People

As a company grows and matures, its culture becomes more independent and more shared. Defining characteristics of collaborators and partners may be spelled out explicitly, but they are confirmed and elaborated through the company's actions. The company's "ideal" employee takes shape through daily interactions and becomes more recognized as an important component of the culture. As Ayah Bdeir explains in describing the culture of littleBits:

"We're a culture of people driven by a passion for our mission and for what we do. Because we're driven by our passion to help others be creative, we accept that a solution can come from anyone—it can come from me or an intern or from user feedback. It doesn't matter. We only care about finding the best solution to the problem."

Of course, some behaviors or qualities that are valued initially lose favor over time. A startup can honestly say, "We will share all job responsibilities." A company of ten thousand employees cannot. On the other hand, some people-centered practices that seem unusual at first can become increasingly important over time.

"

The thing I have learned at IBM is that culture is everything.
Louis V. Gerstner, Jr.

"

Companies that promoted work-life balance used to be considered naive or New Age. But in this "always on" era, work and home life blend.

Creating an environment that acknowledges and respects this significant lifestyle shift attracts top talent who increasingly include company culture in a job evaluation. For some companies this means allowing babies at work; for others it means allowing pets. For still others it means allowing flexible work hours, unlimited vacation days, or educational support. Regardless of the specifics, these once-ridiculed considerations now enjoy much wider acceptance.

Ambiance

A DEO can obsess over the physical environment and office ambiance because she sees them as proxies for cultural values. She knows that the office space influences everyone's mood and mindset on a daily basis. She knows that the lobby makes a first impression on visitors and that conference rooms communicate the company's attitude toward collaboration. She knows that the company's brand isn't limited to its logo, website, or packaging; it can be communicated in the office layout, in the whiteboard pen colors, in the noise level.

Because of this, a DEO may spend months searching for the right office space. She may fret over the food or restroom supplies. She may lie awake rethinking the company email signature—not to get it perfect, but to ensure that it accurately communicates the company's core attributes.

Evolution

As the culture becomes ingrained and widely embraced, the truckload of details that shapes it will no longer need a DEO's constant oversight. An employee handbook may document the ideals, but the culture is reinforced without a rulebook. Over time, stakeholders can sense if something is out of sync with the company's norms. They'll point out discrepancies and add complementary elements. They'll become the keepers of the culture.

Strong company cultures evolve and change over time. DEOs know that a company culture can't stay fixed, but instead must respond to external changes as well as internal pressures. Each crisis, each opportunity is a chance to examine the company culture. Perhaps it can provide immediate and clear guidance. Perhaps it fuels heated debates. Perhaps it is silent. If it's been thoughtfully articulated and widely shared, the corporate culture finds a seat at every meeting.

Workouts to help you build company culture

Act it out.

Even if it hasn't been articulated, your company culture exists. To clarify it or make it more active, integrate it into your daily activities. Consciously evoke it when making decisions. Push its boundaries to see where it's weak. Identify areas of confusion or conflicting values and ask for clarification.

Be seen.

Make company culture more visible. Post signs that reflect important tenets. Add reminders of preferred behavior. Post photos of people who embody the company culture.

Listen well.

Conduct "listening tours" in which you meet stakeholders or customers and hear their stories about the company. Allow yourself only to ask questions. Don't defend or correct—just listen and see the company from another's point of view.

Look around.

Make a point of learning about other companies' cultures. Review employee handbooks posted on the web. Compare notes.

Go elsewhere.

If the company culture conflicts with your values, consider finding another job. You're unlikely to find fulfillment in an organization whose goals you don't support, no matter how much they pay you.

GO DEEPER

Grow: How Ideals Power Growth and Profit at the World's Greatest Companies by Jim Stengel
Absolute Honesty by by Larry Johnson and Bob Phillips
The Designful Company: How to Build a Culture of Nonstop Innovation by Marty Neumeier

A DEO learns early to keep his employees happy. A happy employee—or for that matter, any stakeholder—can improve all aspects of a company. Adequate wages, a manageable workload, and a safe setting are fundamental, but not enough.

Perks like performance bonuses, 401(k) matching funds, and extra personal time certainly matter to an employee. But attracting and keeping talent—particularly creative talent and young professionals—is more of an art than an HR expense.

Some employees may want a less traditional work schedule, arguing that they are more productive late at night or on weekends. Some may want to work from home occasionally or work outside or work from their favorite table at Starbucks. Some may need time in the morning to adjust to the work environment. Others may need a nap at midday or a clothing allowance to upgrade from hoodies. Some may need daycare while others need time off to care for aging parents. Some seek help taking off weight while others want help taking on a mortgage.

If you're a traditional CEO, reading this list angers you. It's entitlement run amok and, if endorsed, a precursor to corporate bankruptcy. But if you're a DEO, you're thinking about how to add flexible schedules, mobile workers, morning breakfasts, a quiet room, and an in-house stylist to your company's list of job perks.

DEOs take the care and feeding of employees seriously for good reason. Ample evidence ties employee care to company performance. A 2012 study by the American Psychological Association found that employees who feel valued are nearly three times more motivated to do their best at work than those who feel unrecognized.[1] The same study found that those who felt valued were much less likely to seek employment elsewhere and much more likely to recommend their workplace to others.

As talent shortages rise to become one of the highest risks companies currently face worldwide,[2] keeping and attracting good people has an immediate and obvious payback. In fact, that payback is what motivated the Parnassus Workplace Fund to invest in companies with outstanding workplaces. They argue that because these companies are able to recruit and retain better employees, they perform at a higher level in terms of innovation, productivity, customer loyalty, and profitability. The fund's five-year return is currently 12.24 percent, compared to the S&P 500 Index at 5.81 percent. That's quite a payback.

95% of Americans consider a job's perks and benefits before deciding to either stay in a position or accept an offer.

Harris Interactive 2012 State of the Workplace: Benefits and Perks Study.

This straightforward *why* of employee care is complemented by an equally straightforward *how*. Employees feel valued when their contributions are recognized, when the company invests in their mentoring and development, and when they feel part of a team. How DEOs offer this recognition, appreciation, and sense of belonging is where care and feeding becomes more dimensional.

> "
> # There are two things people want more than sex and money: recognition and praise.
> Mary Kay Ash
> "

Custom care

In addition to establishing fair and equitable compensation, DEOs are quick to offer acknowledgment, useful feedback, and even something as simple as knowing an employee's name. They're also adept at conceiving nonmonetary rewards with customized appeal.

Every community differs in what it considers a perk. For some, extra time off is coveted. For others, a good-quality office chair makes the difference. We've seen companies offer dry cleaning services, babysitting, in-office health care, nap rooms, on-site massages, gym memberships, personal trainers, monthly BBQs, spontaneous ski trips, outdoor meetings—imagine anything that could make an employee smile and it's probably been offered by a DEO.

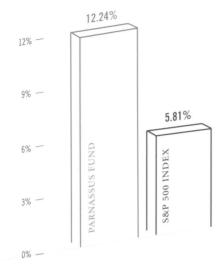

Investing in companies with outstanding workplaces allows the Parnassus Fund to excel over the S&P 500 Index.

Parnassus Fund Quarterly Report. March 2013.

The point is not to be more creative, but to be relevant. DEOs know what their employees and stakeholders value, and they seek to provide it if they can.

Camaraderie

An important part of being a team member is fellowship. This sense of belonging helps coordinate actions, encourage collaboration, and sustain members through downturns and rough patches. A DEO can't force fellowship. It develops over time and with experience, but it can be facilitated. One surprisingly simple means is through food.

Throughout history, shared meals have brought families and communities together. Translated to a company, food can be the great equalizer that creates an experience of shared culture and values.

Visit any technology giant's campus and you'll find an emphasis on the social value of food. Cafeterias offer restaurant quality food at subsidized prices. Yes, companies like Microsoft, Google, and Amazon want to keep their employees working and on the premises, but they also want them to share ideas and knowledge across departments and levels. Likewise, DEOs see food as a platform for collaboration and an inexpensive way to say, "We care about you."

Continual learning

With the advent of online learning and the proliferation of training courses, any employee can pick up new skills. DEOs encourage this by making it more readily available or covering its cost. Simply having a library or allowing employees to access online resources sends a message that learning is valued.

Nathan Shedroff founded a program at California College of the Arts to teach business leadership based on design principles. His Design MBA (DMBA) program exemplifies the productive integration of learning in the workplace. The two-year, graduate-level degree program attracts students from around the world, many of whom are sent by their employers. The class schedule is designed to accommodate students' full-time employment by condensing class time into one long weekend per month. The course assignments are similarly developed to integrate students' learning on systems thinking, sustainability, ethics, and meaningful decision making with the realities they face at work. As a result, the DMBA is producing potential DEOs who return to their companies with expanded networks, enlightened perspectives, and actionable ideas.

1 American Psychological Association. 2012. Psychologically Healthy Workplace Program. http://www.apaexcellence.org
2 Lloyd's. 2011. Lloyd's Risk Index. http://www.lloyds.com/news-and-insight/risk-insight/lloyds-risk-index

Workouts to improve your care and feeding skills

Give a nod.

Develop the habit of acknowledging fellow workers regularly. Compliment a recent accomplishment or a promotion. Point out a notable performance. Applaud a strong presentation. Appreciate a good hair day.

Feed others.

Next time you're dreading a meeting where people tend to sit passively or waste time, arrange to provide food and see what happens. Try menu items that can provoke conversation, like fortune cookies, odd-ingredient pizzas, lesser-known fruit, or exotic desserts.

Learn together.

Take an online course with a group of coworkers. Try to find a skill that will directly benefit your next project or collaboration. Alternatively, find a class that has seemingly nothing to do with your job and then see if you can apply what you learn. No one guessed that calligraphy would be an essential course in the education of Steve Jobs—but it was.

Find perks.

Do research to learn which nonmonetary benefits are gaining popularity in your industry or region. Interview your coworkers to see if any appeal to them. Once you have your evidence, see if your company will embrace new benefits for a trial period. At worst, it won't work, but if it does, you may have a new competitive advantage in attracting talent.

GO DEEPER

Love 'em or Lose 'em: Getting Good People to Stay by Beverly L. Kaye
Managing with Carrots by Adrian Gostick and Chester Elton
The Carrot Principle by Adrian Gostick and Chester Elton
First, Break All the Rules by Marcus Buckingham and Curt Coffman

PLACE MATTERS

It's no accident that the traditional workplace is a flat land of bland, subservient cubicles ringed by the more formal offices of executives. Give a DEO even a modest budget and she will tear down the walls, open up the space, and amp up the color.

Traditional environments were designed to reinforce hierarchical management, linear problem solving, and controlled communications. They still do. A centralized boardroom usually crouches in the corner, meting out power and prestige to those allowed access. The beige, nondescript lobby serves as a moat, warding off unauthorized outsiders. The overall layout segregates departments and discourages spontaneous collaboration.

A DEO redesigns her environments to reflect her company's culture. This is not an act of entrepreneurial rebellion or even personal expression. A DEO knows that place matters. She builds work environments to support her company's distinct processes and people.

Environments influence us, often in ways that we barely perceive, but that nonetheless register on a brain-wave test. Designing workspaces that support employees, promote creativity, communicate a company's culture, and broadcast its brand is a tall order, but also a smart priority.

A colorful, imaginative, and open lobby welcomes stakeholders, clients, and visitors into the heart of Hot Studio.

The basics

Improving basic considerations like lighting, climate control, chair structure, and noise levels can improve productivity, lower stress, and increase job satisfaction.[1] Adding more open space spurs collaboration and spontaneous idea sharing. Smaller, more informal conference rooms with whiteboards or writable surfaces inspire brainstorming, visualizing, and ad hoc meetings. Even greenery plays a positive role in supporting and enhancing workplace activities.[2]

An open lobby that welcomes visitors into the heart of the company sends an important message to clients, vendors, customers, and other external communities.

The corner office still beckons to the traditional CEO, promising a veneer of status, but a DEO finds no security in sitting in a corner. She

prefers a spot in the middle of the action, with no walls or doors between her and the rest of the company. Being productive in the middle of day-to-day chaos is a valuable lesson to model. When she needs privacy, she goes to a small conference room or a restaurant or some other reserved space. But when she's in the office, she's *in* the office.

Added touches

In addition to endorsing open, collaborative environments, a DEO respects the usefulness of comfort—not comfort as in ease or luxury, but rather homeyness. Traditional office environments can be artificial and cold. The sterile settings remind employees that they are away from home and other locations they enjoy or associate with their well-being. By adding decorative or communal touches—couches, throw pillows, soft lighting, quiet rooms, or social spaces—a DEO can increase employees' appreciation of the workspace and consequently, their job satisfaction.[3]

Another added touch that DEOs believe contributes more value than cost is integrating a company's brand identity throughout its workplace. The company invests in creating a memorable identity and experience online and in numerous other platforms—why not use the physical environment as well? Corporate colors are the easiest expression to add, followed by signage and related decor. But furniture, layout, space allocation, lighting, and "extras" like a kitchen, all say a great deal about what the company values. Done well, a branded office can communicate as forcefully and coherently as a well-placed ad or well-designed website.

By adding decorative or communal touches a DEO can increase employees' appreciation of the workplace and their job satisfaction.

"

My ideas usually come not at my desk writing but in the midst of living.
Anaïs Nin

"

Other places

While a DEO values the power of office environments, she also knows their limitations. A space devoted to productivity and concerted effort—no matter how attractively and smartly designed—may actually inhibit creativity and inventiveness.

In an article exploring the neuroscience of insight, Jonah Lehrer explains that our brains are more likely to find and accept new ideas when we're relaxed and not attuned.[4] Trying to force originality in an office environment may be the equivalent of taking an anti-inspiration pill.

It's these findings on the genesis of the "aha!" moment that helps a DEO approve a brainstorming offsite in Yosemite. Or accommodate an employee working outside the office. Or schedule a walking meeting. Relaxation, daydreaming, and laughter are legitimate ingredients of innovation. If the current environment isn't nurturing them, a good DEO will find more fertile ground.

1 Atkinson, Martin. "The positive impact of office design." *FMLink*.
2 "The Benefits of Plants in the Workplace." *WorkDesign* magazine. July 2012. http://workdesign.co/2012/07/the-benefits-of-plants-in-the-workplace/
3 O'Neill, Michael. 2010. Generational Preferences: A Glimpse into the Future Office. Knoll Workplace Research.
4 Lehrer, Jonah. 2008. "The Eureka Hunt: Why Do Good Ideas Come to Us When They Do?" *The New Yorker*, July28. http://www.newyorker.com/reporting/2008/07/28/080728fa_fact_lehrer

Workouts to help you build a better workspace

Get personal.

Start by making your own office more personal. Add visuals that inspire you, toys that make you laugh, flowers, and personal mementos. Add anything that helps others relate better to you as a person or that helps you feel more at home and engaged.

Pin it up.

Find signage that relates to your company's brand or culture and post it throughout the office. In Maria's studio, the infamous "Be Calm" signs were pervasive, each customized to suit the area. In Christopher's office, large profiles of "everyday" people adorned the walls.

Sign out.

Invite collaboration by making it clear when you need be alone and when you're open to interruption. This can be as simple as using a small red flag to indicate that you don't want to be disturbed. Just don't overuse it.

"OOO"

Find places out of the office where you can relax while continuing to work. Hot Studio had "Conference Room K." The K was short for Katie O'Brien's, the bar next door where colleagues could gather for drinks and impromptu collaborations. Your alternate office could be a café, a park bench, or even a quiet corner in a museum.

Lounge around.

If your office has an unused conference room or similar private setting, see if you can turn it into a room for casual conversation or brief breaks. Fill it with books or toys or provocative puzzles. Encourage others to visit "the lounge" when they feel unproductive or anxious.

GO DEEPER

Workplace by Design: Mapping the High-Performance Workscape by Franklin Becker and Fritz Steele
Best of Office Architecture and Design by Cindy Allen
Make Space: How to Set the Stage for Creative Collaboration by Scott Doorley and Scott Witthoft
I Wish I Worked There! by Kursty Groves and Will Knight

Mark Dwight

President and CEO of Rickshaw Bagworks

Mark bounds into his office in San Francisco's Dogpatch neighborhood like a ten-year-old kid. On paper, he's the founder and CEO of Rickshaw Bagworks, a company inspired by creative energy, urban cycling, and a strong set of humanistic, environmental, and social values. In person, he's a happy DEO who's built his dream manufacturing "fort" and plays there daily with his friends.

We interviewed Dwight in the midst of the bustling warehouse where Rickshaw makes and sells its bags. Surrounded by the sounds of his business, he explained a career filled with equal measures of passion and iteration.

As a child, what did you think you'd be when you grew up?

When I was a young kid, I thought I was going to be a paleontologist. I was a big rock collector, stamp collector, and fossil hunter. I spent a lot of time kind of solo, marching around in a creek behind a tennis club that my parents belonged to. I even found a woolly mammoth tusk!

But I've always had some entrepreneurial instinct. Whether by birth or by nature or nurture, I felt bound to be an entrepreneur. My father was an early Silicon Valley entrepreneur. He founded the first laser company in 1962, so I grew up around Silicon Valley, startup companies, and the notion of being the master of your own destiny.

Do you think of yourself as creative?

I'm sort of like this left-handed engineer. I took mechanical engineering as my major at Stanford, partially because I never regarded myself as artistic enough to be a designer. Even though I write every day and I sketch, I never fancied myself as an artist. Although, ironically, I find some consolation in these books that reveal the notes of famous designers and architects—they can't draw worth crap either.

Maybe a designer is sort of this mid-place between an engineer and artist. In collaboration with a junior designer and the rest of my staff, I really do all the design work here. I come up

with the initial idea, then we start working through it. It's always a sort of iterative process. You need other people. It takes a team.

Were you confident in your creativity at an early age?

In 1982, when I graduated, the design program at Stanford was in its infancy. Electrical engineers looked down on mechanical engineers. Mechanical engineers looked down on designers. That was engineering for poets. Design didn't have as much respect back then. David Kelley was actually an assistant professor in my ME103 class when I was at Stanford.

"

A designer is sort of this mid-place between an engineer and artist.

"

I felt that if I was going to get a real job in Silicon Valley and do right by my parents for the money they were spending to send me to Stanford, I should get an engineering degree.

I didn't really get into design until I ran a small startup in 1992. I hired Lunar and let them do what they wanted to do. I was creative, but I wanted to let the designers do their thing. We came out with a really good result. When I left that startup, I spent some time with Lunar in business development. I figured I could sell design because I had been a good client. I met Brett Lovelady at Lunar and figured we were smart

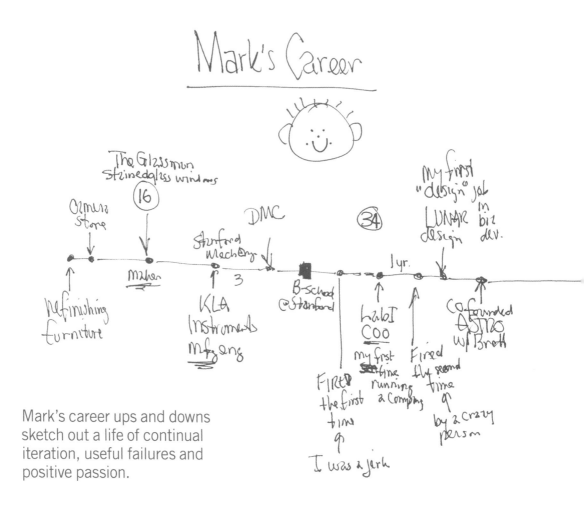

Mark's Career

(handwritten timeline labels)
The Glassman Stainedglass windows
16
Ozmun Store
DMC
34
my first "design" job LUNAR design in biz dev.
Refinishing furniture
Maher
Stanford Machinery
3
KLA Instruments Mfg eng
B-school @ Stanford
1 yr.
Labl COO
Co-founded ASTRO w/ Broth
my first time running a company
Fired the second time
FIRED the first time ©
by a crazy person
I was a jerk

Mark's career ups and downs sketch out a life of continual iteration, useful failures and positive passion.

enough to run our own design firm. Be careful what you wish for! So we started Astro Studios.

Two years later, I really wanted to make stuff. I knew I had this gravitational pull of wanting to make things.

How do you recognize creativity in others?

I think that the most important trait for being creative is being open-minded and wanting to experience the world. When I worked in teams and had a budget to send people out to do design research or send people to the factory in China, I would tell them to take an extra day. What's it to us? We're already paying your airfare and most of your expenses, so take an extra day and just experience the place.

I think most good designers are in and of the world. They see all the things that are going on around them: the things that work, the things that don't. It's the synthesis of these observations that makes you a good designer. I love going to trade shows that are completely outside my realm of business because I see things I don't expect. I could go to a building conference and

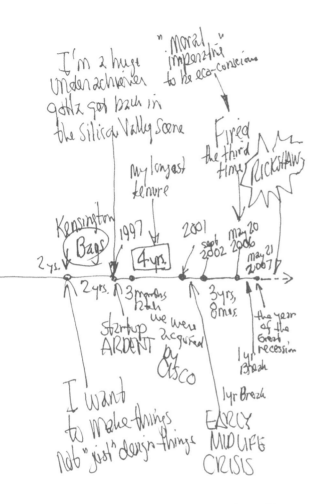

When did you first realize you could lead?

My first opportunity to lead was running a small startup with ten people in it. I really enjoyed that. I felt a great deal of freedom, but I was being managed by a chairman and a board, so I was always aware that this was sort of a false sense of independence. I was beholden to someone else. Rickshaw's a manifestation of my personality and my vision and my values and my goals. It's my dream.

What's your leadership style now?

I like to think that I'm realistic. I'm self-directed, but I'm aware of my surroundings and the people around me, especially. And I appreciate the need to have my team participate and buy into the things that we do here. While it's ultimately my responsibility, my decision, I don't enjoy working by myself. I'm perfectly comfortable by myself and spend time alone, but I prefer to work with a team.

Did you overcome any hurdles in developing your career and building your business?

Oh, I'm not good at working for other people and that has been my Achilles' heel. I mean, I've been fired three times in my career. So I'm proof that there's life after being fired.

The first time, I was working for a company and I didn't like my manager. I wore it on my sleeve and ultimately I got fired for not getting along with people. The second time I got fired, I was actually working with a mad scientist in

see materials that I never expected. I could go to an equipment conference and say, "Wow, that's weird. I never even thought of that." It just opens your eyes.

I also believe that design is about connecting dots in novel ways. It's not necessarily about inventing something from scratch. It's about tweaking something or putting the elements together in ways that they haven't been mixed up before. It doesn't take much. I mean, in my business, some of the most interesting innovations are minor. You just have to find someone's blind spot—something that someone never thought of before.

a start-up. It turns out the guy was actually certifiably insane. The last time was with Timbuk2. I was completely misaligned in values with my new investors. We became financially focused and less brand focused, less creative—it became obvious that we weren't going to work well together. And they held all the cards. So it was their way or the highway. I think each of those times I really came face-to-face with the idea that I didn't want to be working for other people.

What I really like about running my own business is that I can just be true to my own values. Business editors ask, "What's the future of Rickshaw?" And I tell them I'm not here to make as many bags as possible. I'm here to make as many bags as necessary to run a small, sustainable business. I don't have any aspiration to be the king of the bag business. What I want to be known for is having started and run a successful business. Success to me is a profitable business that provides meaningful jobs for my team of people and provides me with a fulfilling and rewarding profession. And obviously pays my bills and everyone else's bills.

Do you have processes or tools that help people collaborate?

I'm a fan of exploring the mild to wild. It's my responsibility to rein it back in when it's time to decide what's within the realm of practicality and financial possibility, but I try not to constrain the situation too much upfront.

I try to use my own thinking outside the box to show people that there are other ways to think of things. My staff generally has trepidation about me going to a TED conference because they know when I came back there will be a flurry of "You can't believe what I saw!

Here's what we should do and here's a bunch of new ideas." They're thinking, "Oh God, like we don't have enough work already."

Certainly one of my challenges is the shiny penny phenomenon. I'm fascinated by the next new thing. I love to start things. I've gotten much better at delegating because I know this now. I'm completely aware that other creative individuals can execute on the ideas that I think are interesting. Now that I have a design assistant, I'll just take it to a certain point and say, "You go figure out that stuff and then come back to me and we'll review it." I don't need to be down in the weeds of the execution anymore.

Are there any traditional management behaviors that you've outlawed at Rickshaw?

We've been conditioned, especially in Silicon Valley, around the concepts of hypergrowth and greatness and billion dollar markets. There's this idea that if it isn't a revolution, it's not worth doing. But I believe that, ultimately, if you're pursuing your passion and doing the great work that you want to do, whether it's revolutionary or a billion dollar opportunity is irrelevant.

For everyone who shoots for the stars, most of them miss. For the ones who are successful, most of the time it's just sheer luck. And you can't go around hoping to win the lottery. We mythologize the serial entrepreneur. The serial entrepreneur really is someone who can't keep up with these hypergrowth companies and gets fired all the time. I think that the tragedy of this kind of Silicon Valley hypergrowth model is that the CEO who can survive that is extraordinarily rare.

"The difficulty is in the doing" is a favorite saying that Mark lives up to each year as he bikes from San Francisco to the TED conference in Long Beach, California.

You open your company to the public for tours. Why?

One of my Markisms is "The difficulty is in the doing." We roll up the doors every day and invite people into our factory to see what we do and how we do it. I think that narrative—the who, what, why, where, and how, being able to show people that we make stuff—is, frankly, one of our biggest assets.

We're not just in the manufacturing business; we're in show business. That show we put on every day is the thing that differentiates us from other bag companies. There are thousands of bag companies. We've tried to create products that have their own look and feel, or silhouette, as we say in the fashion business. But at the end of the day, one of the biggest things I'm selling is the fact that you can come here and see it. You can

know us, the maker, not just the marketer. That's why I also started the association SFMade. I really felt that we should celebrate this noble pursuit of making things.

When you're gone from the scene, what three things do you want to be known for?

Generosity and passion—well, and integrity. You're nothing without that. There's no job worth winning, there's no mistake worth covering at the expense of personal integrity and at the expense of honesty.

Cheaters never win. They never do. They win in the short-term, but they never win in the long-term. And it's just a bad way to get ahead.

photo courtesy of dynamosquito

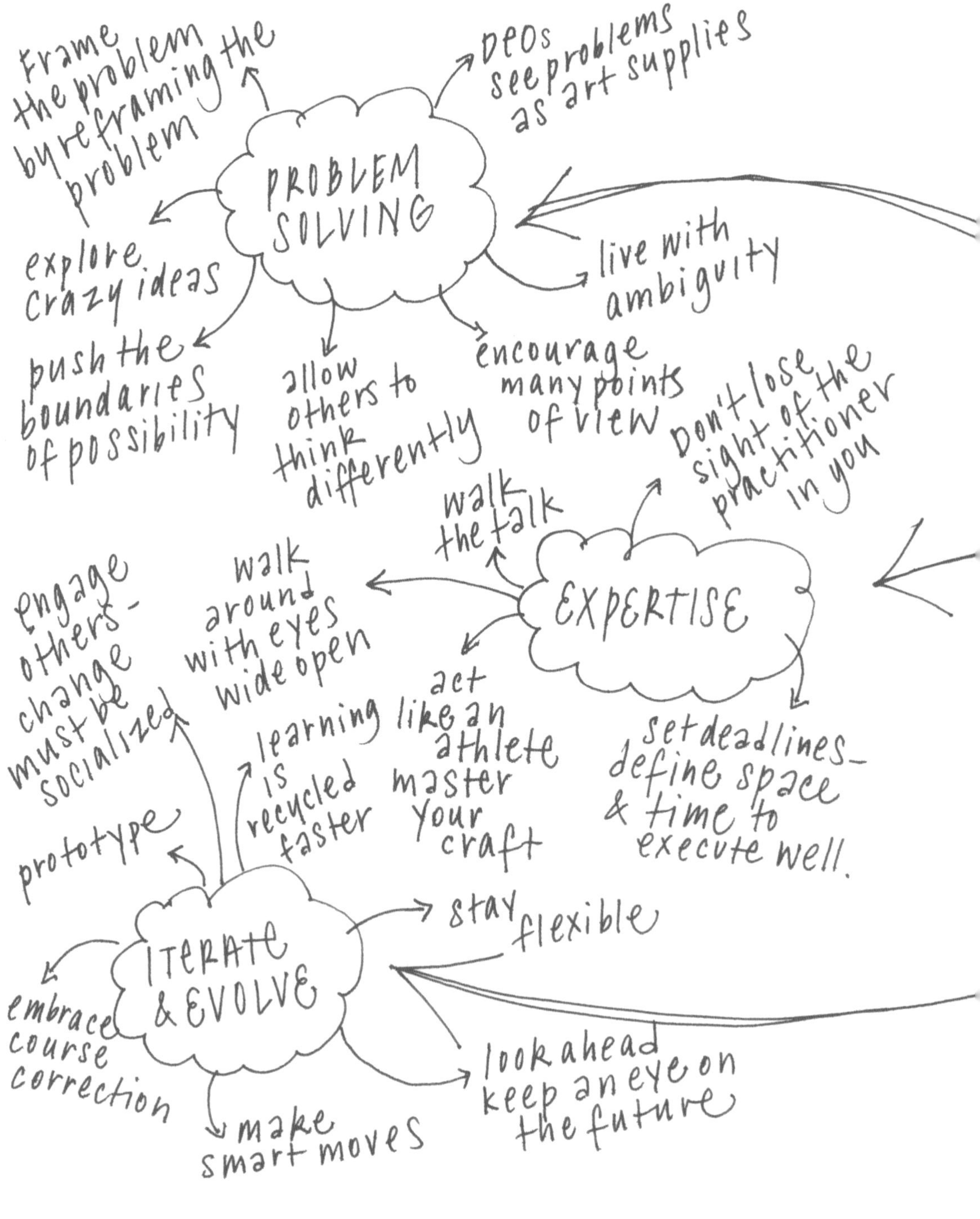

frame the problem by reframing the problem

DEOs see problems as art supplies

PROBLEM SOLVING

explore crazy ideas

live with ambiguity

push the boundaries of possibility

allow others to think differently

encourage many points of view

Don't lose sight of the practitioner in you

walk the talk

engage others - change must be socialized

walk around with eyes wide open

EXPERTISE

act like an athlete

learning is recycled faster

master your craft

set deadlines - define space & time to execute well.

prototype

ITERATE & EVOLVE

stay flexible

embrace course correction

make smart moves

look ahead keep an eye on the future

do

PLAYFUL WORK
- makes us smarter
- an antidote to stress
- is contagious
- opens new communication channels

PERMISSION TO FAIL
- failure = learning
- acknowledge mistakes
- share accountability
- make small bets
- solicit feedback

POSITIVE PASSION
- love what you do
- be optimistic
- stay the course & keep your eye on the prize
- builds resistance through downturns
- stay open to input & alternative viewpoints

POSITIVE PASSION

Each year, hordes of new graduates pour into the traditional business world obediently following the dreams of their parents. Within months, many are looking for a way out as they realize this is not their passion. DEOs are among the first to bolt.

Early in his career, a DEO discovers that he must follow his heart and not the crowd. While he might make it through graduate school studying topics that don't resonate, his patience for the irrelevant shrinks to zero at work. He knows instinctively that his only chance of success is to pursue a passion.

If he enjoys his work and finds it fully engaging and challenging, he'll give it more time and energy. If he's personally involved and emotionally committed, he'll have the push to move forward and the pull to attract others.

But passion alone is not sufficient for a DEO. Without the tempering influence of a positive attitude, passion can easily take up residence in the land of "too crazy for me." Because he's dependent on the skills and support of others to bring his dream to life, a DEO is careful to express his passion in a way that is engaging and collaborative.

Passion's benefits are compounded and exponential when conveyed in a positive manner. Others feel a DEO's zeal and long to be on his team. If they can't join, they'll seek to support him financially or emotionally. At the very least, a positively passionate DEO will gain visibility, and his message will spread more quickly and pervasively.

Bryan Stevenson demonstrated the power of positive passion when he spoke at the TED conference in 2012. Few in the audience had ever heard of the middle-aged public interest lawyer who has dedicated his career to helping the poor, the incarcerated, and the condemned. But from his opening explanation, "I spend most of my time in jails, in prisons, on death row," to his closing plea, "I think that's the orientation that we have to change," the crowd could not look away. He not only received the longest standing ovation in TED's history, but also gathered over $1 million in pledges on the spot. More than one million people have viewed the video of his talk.

Despite Stevenson's example, even positive passion doesn't guarantee success. What it does guarantee is better-quality work, increased creativity, more empathy, and greater job satisfaction.[1] These promises are compelling enough for DEOs to role model positive passion for stakeholders and endorse it as a fundamental behavior throughout their organizations. DEOs urge employees to follow their hearts in a manner that's open, resilient, and optimistic.

Stay open

Passion has a habit of narrowing perspective. A DEO's attention is channeled into his singular focus. While this prevents distractions, it can blind him to fresh advice and cautious counsel. To counter this tendency, DEOs try to stay open to others' input and alternative viewpoints. This takes practice.

Who feels "energized" or "inspired" by unexpected challenges?

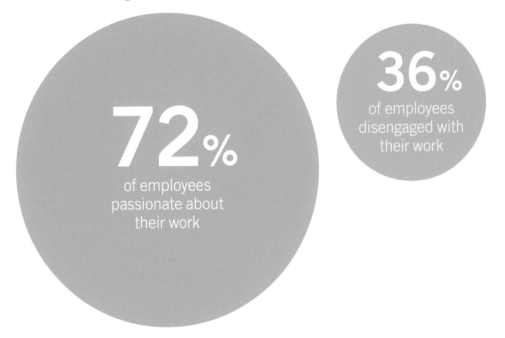

72% of employees passionate about their work

36% of employees disengaged with their work

Deloitte 2011 Shift Index www.deloitte.com/us/workerpassion

"

When genuine passion moves you, say what you've got to say, and say it hot.
D. H. Lawrence

"

Staying open means being willing to review contradictory data, hear criticism, look beyond normal boundaries, and resist quick judgments. It means sharing key developments, underlying assumptions, and factual updates.

Staying open doesn't mean starting fresh each day with no preconceptions or permanent understandings. That's an excellent movie plot but a poor way to accomplish anything meaningful.

Build resilience

Resilience, in the context of passion, is the ability to persevere through the inevitable downturns of dream development. It's the ability to accept changes that are unwelcome or outside our control. It's the ability to regroup, reassess, and reignite passions rather than give up and go home. In practical terms, it's the ability to experience bankruptcy, product failure, personal embarrassment, and your dog dying all in the same week, then wake up on Monday feeling the best is yet to come.

DEOs probably have a natural tendency toward resilience, but they build it in the workplace by modeling it and by direct coaching and caring. By sharing his time and showing empathy, a DEO shepherds others through the bleak periods. By staying open to pivots and optimistic about the company's potential, he paints a picture of the future that's engaging enough to make today's bad news seem minor and temporary. He is able to point out the hidden benefits in each downturn, the silver lining in any rejection.

Be optimistic

Scratch the surface of resilience and you'll find optimism. The hope for a better day, another chance, or a more positive outcome is an expression of optimism. It's the consoling voice that tells us to pick up the pieces and try again. It's your mom saying, "Think about the good things in life."

Optimism fuels a DEO's belief that he can overcome obstacles or solve problems. A hopeful perspective keeps a DEO open to other possibilities and new options. It helps him believe there is new potential created every day and that his company will be the next one to hit it big.

An organization filled with optimistic, passionate stakeholders is one that grows and flourishes even in a down economy.[2] Any DEO who's survived a recession or a market crash knows that optimism (and a small cash buffer) is the primary difference between "down and out" and "up and over."

---

1 Vacharkulksemsuk, Tanya, Leslie E. Sekerka, and Barbara L. Fredrickson. 2011. "Establishing a Positive Emotional Climate to Create 21st-Century Organizational Change."

2 Amabile, Teresa, and Steven Kramer. 2011. "Do Happier People Work Harder?" New York Times, September 3. http://www.nytimes.com/2011/09/04/opinion/sunday/do-happier-people-work-harder.html?_r=0.

Workouts to increase your positive passion

Go back.

Revisit the passions of your childhood. Think back to the activities that captivated you when you were young and see if they still hold your attention. These early passions are often what drive us later in life. If your current career lacks ambition or enthusiasm, perhaps it's because you left it behind in the fourth grade.

Draw pictures.

Make your passion visible. Surround yourself with signs, symbols, and images that indicate what you love and why you love it. Integrate your goals into these visuals.

Skip lunch.

If your current job or company does not drive you, find time every day to work on a project that does. This may mean giving up your lunch hour. It may mean getting less sleep. Both conditions are good tests of your commitment. If you won't lose sleep over a project you say you love, it's probably not really your passion.

Work it out.

Take a working vacation. If you're a programmer but you really want to be a cheese-maker, spend your next vacation learning to make cheese. You'll either enjoy the work or quickly learn this is not really for you.

Follow leaders.

Follow the adventures of others chasing their dream. Read their blogs and tweets or view their videos. Spend enough time studying them to recognize the signs of passionate pursuit. Learn how they handle setbacks and how they overcome hurdles.

GO DEEPER

The Fred Factor by Mark Sanborn and John C. Maxwell
Work with Passion: How to Do What You Love for a Living by Nancy Anderson
Make the Impossible Possible by Bill Strickland and Vince Rause

EXPERTISE

A DEO is a practitioner who never loses touch with her craft. She's called on clients. She's built prototypes. She's filled out expense forms. She's bought pizza and delivered it to employees working overtime. She does this and more to get as close as possible to her company's values, people, and operations.

She doesn't have delegation or micromanagement issues. She knows that being "close in" lets her act faster, more accurately, and better than being "hands-off."

A DEO also enjoys the work. It's why she started the business or worked her way up. It's why she continues to innovate and evolve, and it's why she promotes the company and its products or services. To complete a task or reach a goal is personally satisfying to a DEO. To see a prototype quickly take shape from the seed of an idea nourishes creativity and rewards risk-taking.

Not all DEOs are designers, but all DEOs have invested considerable time and energy in developing a skill relevant to some aspect of their business. Where a traditional CEO might relate to numbers on a spreadsheet that track recent sales or profitability, a DEO relates to the look, feel, or experience of the company's products and services. She is intimately involved in the product development process, not just at the level of strategy, but also where the company interacts with its customers. She models this involvement to everyone in the company, broadcasting that even the highest-level executive has skills common to the product team.

A DEO's close involvement in her company's actual work process can help create and strengthen ties with stakeholders and increase their confidence in her. When employees see a leader who can walk the talk, they're more likely to trust her instincts, knowing that those instincts are grounded in a deep knowledge of the business.

Rather than rise above her expertise as she gains power and authority, a DEO practices her expertise as part of running the business. Mark Zuckerberg's ability to code enhances his credibility with his engineers and contributes to the growth and development of Facebook. Oprah Winfrey's interviewing skills keep her in the spotlight. Jeff Bezos buying *The Washington Post* suggests he's still engaged in reading.

Aside from contributing to the product development process, a DEO's expertise can serve as a superpower that helps her look ahead. Her command of a subject helps her see meaningful patterns of information that go unnoticed by others. She can retrieve relevant knowledge more easily and apply it to problem solving more efficiently.[1]

Through her relentless commitment to improvement and her added powers of expertise, a DEO urges her company to constantly better itself or, if needed, to reinvent. When Chris Anderson acquired the TED Conference in 2001, it was a small, elite annual gathering of wealthy business people. His passion

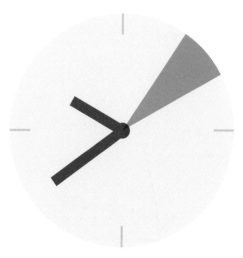

A leader should spend 5–10% of his time doing the actual work of his employees.

Source info to come.Source info to come.Source info to come.Source info to come.Source info to come.

to spread good ideas combined with his expertise as a publisher transformed the conference into a media platform that now reaches over a billion viewers. Where others saw only a high-status conference, Anderson—through his expertise—saw an opportunity for a global media revolution.

Building and maintaining expertise without becoming rigid is a daunting task, but a DEO has ways of rising to the challenge by emulating athletes, anchors, and amateurs.

Be an athlete

Regardless of the sport, no athlete can simply think her way to the top. She can read or watch a thousand hours of expert ski techniques, but improvement won't come without considerable time on the slopes putting those lessons to the test.

"

We are what we repeatedly do. Excellence, then, is not an act, but a habit.

Aristotle

"

Similarly, a DEO values training, inspiration, coaching, and any learning she can get, but she knows that taking action is the only way to develop new skills or enhance those she already has. She makes sure her leadership duties do not consign her to a string of meetings and conferences, but instead allow her to continue to practice her craft and perfect her skills.

Like any ambitious athlete, a DEO sets goals that exceed her current capabilities. She commits to practice her skills repeatedly and to improve them in any way she can. If she's at the top of her game, she tries to add more flair and style, or she ventures into new territory.

When Malcolm Gladwell suggested in his book *Outliers: The Story of Success* that expertise requires a minimum of 10,000 hours of practice, DEOs rejoiced. Finally, someone had identified a clear goal within reach of a dedicated DEO.

Be an anchor

Most people hate deadlines. They're the solid wall into which our boundless capability crashes and dies. A DEO has a different perspective. She views deadlines like a news anchor—routine, inevitable, and ultimately beneficial.

Deadlines are master choreographers, defining the space and time a DEO has to create a solution or address a problem. Instead of killing her capability, it shapes and defines it to fit the allotted time. It also gives her a chance to over deliver, something a DEO never tires of doing.

Spend some time with a DEO and you're sure to hear the question, "When is this due?" It's not the precursor to complaint. It's part of defining the problem and understanding the constraints within which she and her team will find a solution.

Be an amateur

Most senior executives pride themselves on their experience and seniority. After all, it's one of the few advantages of aging. But a DEO forces herself to become a novice—repeatedly—by learning new skills, trying new roles, or participating in new environments.

Being a novice gives her the experience of a "beginner's mind," an open, enthusiastic embrace of new approaches or perspectives. Being a novice also gives her a chance to examine habitual behaviors or cognitive ruts she may have developed. This mindset can introduce her to new patterns or insights that she's unable to see as an expert. It can renew her vision and refresh her enthusiasm.

---

1 Bransford, John D., ed. 2000. How People Learn: Brain, Mind, Experience, and School, expanded ed. Washington, DC: National Academy Press. http://www.napedu/openbook/0309070368/html/31html, copyright, 2000 The National Academy of Sciences.

Workouts to strengthen your expertise

Take lessons.

You're never too expert for lessons. Sign up for classes that extend and improve your area of expertise. Now that so many courses are available online, there's really no excuse. Hire a more advanced teacher to take you to the next level of skill. Push yourself to risk failure as a way of developing more capability.

Live to learn.

Develop the habit of learning something new every day. Read an article, watch a video, attend a lecture, ask questions of a friend or colleague, read the online comments of strangers, or view photos from places you've never visited. Don't think of these as lessons—think of them as a daily gulp of new knowledge.

Speak up.

Share your knowledge as widely as you can. Nothing improves expertise like being public about it. Start a blog or simply tweet regularly on a subject you can claim some expertise about. Don't worry about being "the best." If you know more about a topic than most, share it.

Find experts.

Hang out with experts more knowledgeable than you, especially those born a decade or more before you. Question them and listen closely. Observe their work. Volunteer to assist them. Seek their counsel.

GO DEEPER

The Talent Code: Greatness Isn't Born. It's Grown. Here's How by Daniel Coyle
Practice Perfect by Doug Lemov, Erica Woolway, and Katie Yezzi
Outliers: The Story of Success by Malcolm Gladwell

PROBLEM SOLVING

No problem. This routine email reply is shorthand for *don't worry, everything's fine.* Taken literally, it's a DEO's worst nightmare. No problem means no opportunity, no challenge, and no chance to wrestle complex, often conflicting details and data into an elegant, meaningful solution.

Problem solving is why DEOs get out of bed in the morning. This drive starts early—for most, in childhood—and compels many of their career decisions. Where traditional managers and leaders view problems as negatives to be minimized, DEOs see problems as art supplies. They choose them carefully and use them to explore and expand their creativity.

Chip Conley built his wildly popular hotel chain, Joie de Vivre, by solving a series of problems. At 26, he bought the rundown Caravan Motor Lodge, a seedy San Francisco property that mostly catered to hookers. Unable to attract tourists because of its bad location, he reached out to travel agents who booked hotels for rock and roll bands, a class of traveler that few hotels wanted.

The musicians flocked to Conley's newly named Phoenix Hotel. Adventure-seeking celebrities soon followed, turning the once modest motel into a cultural hot spot. Conley went on to renovate a number of rundown hotels, following the same process: he framed the problem, diverged from standard thinking, and let the solution take shape.

Framing the problem

For a DEO, solving a problem starts with framing it. This sounds easier than it is. Framing a problem means identifying exactly what's going wrong and what may be causing it. Done correctly, frameworks create useful boundaries that define the parameters of success without prescribing the solution. Simplistic, rushed framing typically results in a simplistic, rushed solution that falls apart in the prototyping phase, fails in pilot tests, or dies in the market.

Some problems resist solution because they're incorrectly framed. A company defines a problem based on its experience and perspective, but a fresh team finds a different, more solvable, way of looking at it. Other problems are too large or unwieldy and need a more manageable scope. Frameworks can break a large problem into smaller pieces more easily understood and addressed.

Developing an effective framework demands close observation and deep understanding. This is where customer interviews, store visits, trend analysis, user videos, and any other means of insight provide vital clues. Ideally these insights are conveyed through a variety of mediums, including photos, videos, stories, sound, and role-playing—the greater the range, the better to engage team members and broaden their perspective. And that broader perspective spurs wider, more divergent thinking about what might work.

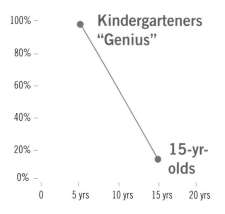

98% percent of kindergarteners scored in the "genius" level of divergent thinking compared to 12% of 15-year-olds.

Breakpoint and Beyond by George Land and Beth Jarman.

Divergent thinking

Divergent thinking—the ability to conceive of many options or alternatives—unlocks creativity and shifts perspective. A DEO practices and encourages divergent thinking to generate the widest exploration of what's possible and to shift that exploration from a linear or rule-bound study to one that's surprising and original.

Divergent thinking considers regulations that could be changed, territory that's unexplored, and products that might be possible. It also produces crazy, half-baked notions without a chance of success. That's part of its charm.

As you might expect, divergent thinking is common among children. In a 2000 study of 1,500 kindergarteners by George Land and Beth Jarman, 98 percent scored in the genius level for divergent thinking. Sadly, their scores declined dramatically as they got older. By the time kids leave school, their divergent thinking skills have been educated out of them.

> "
>
> # If I had an hour to solve a problem, I'd spend 55 minutes thinking about the problem and 5 minutes thinking about solutions.
>
> Albert Einstein
>
> "

In business, leaders are likewise rewarded for decisiveness and "right" answers. Speculative queries that wander through a forest of what-ifs are considered only appropriate for daydreamers and the unfocused. But DEOs know that converging on an answer too quickly often favors existing beliefs and experiences and discounts new ideas before they can be fully considered. To overcome the tendency for convergence, a DEO seeks a truly diverse group of collaborators and colleagues.

A team of hipsters may be open-minded, but its members share a similar outlook and lifestyle, even if they are of different genders and ethnicities. A DEO populates her company and work groups with people who experience the world in different ways: low income, high income, disabled, older, teens, conservatives, radicals, artists, technicians, musicians. She guides this eclectic ensemble like a jam session—coaxing the best performance from each person, and hoping for an outcome that transcends each individual's input.

Living with ambiguity

While a DEO prizes clarity, she knows that some problems require a period of ambiguity. She learns, usually through early experience, that some solutions need to gestate. They need to float in a back channel of the brain before they're ready to jump, fully formed, into the conscious mind or onto a whiteboard. But trust in the unknown is not a common trait among business people. Often the greater challenge is getting a team of deadline-driven collaborators to wait patiently while a solution takes shape in their collective unconscious.

While people accept ambiguity in many parts of life, it's often more problematic in an office. Perhaps because work appears to be more rational, we expect less gray and more black-and-white. Even if a DEO could make everything certain and exact, she wouldn't because she respects the magic of ambiguity and its ability to sort out details without deliberate effort.

To help gain acceptance of ambiguity's role in problem solving, a DEO shifts the team's focus from the solution to the process of solving. She reminds the group that problem solving is a journey that's never quite complete. She emphasizes iterations and eschews perfection. She urges the team to play with the potential solutions, rotate them, mix them up, and post them for comment. She mandates recreational time and sleep as integral parts of the process.

Workouts to make you a better problem solver

Map it out.

Learn to mindmap. We used MindMode for this book, but there are plenty of other good options to try, or you can use pencil and paper. Next time you're faced with a problem, try to mindmap the elements that caused the problem. Return to the map repeatedly to add more insights. Look for areas where information is missing and let that guide your research.

Invite trouble.

Invite outsiders to any brainstorming sessions. Make sure at least one person in the session is a rabble-rouser or troublemaker who's sure to fight against the status quo. Keep a bowl of M&Ms on the table. If energy starts to lag or the room grows silent, start throwing the M&Ms at the troublemaker and let him take it from there.

Solve together.

Gather your colleagues at work and solve the Marshmallow Challenge. In eighteen minutes, teams compete to build the tallest freestanding structure out of twenty sticks of spaghetti, one yard of tape, one yard of string, and one marshmallow. The marshmallow needs to be on top. Divergent thinking pays off.

Make time.

Anytime you create a project schedule, add in time for divergent thinking and ambiguity. Use titles like "creative exploration" and "internal validation," even though what you mean is "spend more time daydreaming about solutions" and "soak in the hot tub for a while."

GO DEEPER

Problem Solving 101: A Simple Book for Smart People by Ken Watanabe
The Thinker's Toolkit: 14 Powerful Techniques for Problem Solving by Morgan D. Jones
The Power of Thinking Differently by Javy W. Galindo
Divergent Thinking (Creativity Research Series) by Mark A. Runco

Steve Gundrum

President, CEO, and Professional Inventor
of Mattson

Steve smiles comfortably and settles into a chair. He has an air of contentment that hides a thirst for discovery and a passion for invention. As CEO of Mattson, one of the country's foremost food research and development labs, he spends his days mixing chemistry and culinary arts.

We talked with Gundrum one afternoon over iced lattes at a local Starbucks. Surrounded by the products and experience of his passion, he described a career that's one part scientist and one part artist—the perfect recipe for a DEO.

As a child, what did you think you'd be when you grew up?

I always wanted to invent. In grade school my neighbor and I made make-believe rocket ships and talked about flying around and picking up our friends.

In sixth grade I designed my idea of a maglev train. It was conceptual, but I figured out all the engineering details. My teacher said it was stupid—that it could never work—but I knew he was wrong because we'd been playing with magnets in class and I understood their properties.

This got me interested in drafting tools. I saved up my money and bought everything I could find: a drafting table, T-bars, mechanical pencils, an architect's ruler. I thought they were so beautiful. I loved looking at them and holding them. I only bought "good stuff" and I used them to draw everything. I drew houses, trains, rocket ships, anything. Everything I drew had to be precise and to scale, with multiple perspectives. I loved starting with a white canvas and creating something.

Do you recall any early childhood experience that shaped your career?

I was about twelve or thirteen and in the Milwaukee airport when I saw a travel poster for Northwest Orient Airlines. The poster turned the U.S. map upside down and flipped it so Florida pointed up and to the left. Then they had overlaid the title "Fly Northwest to Florida" (Steve draws the poster from memory). I remember being struck by the sheer cleverness and creativity of this concept. It was a profound moment that turned on my interest in being creative—that this was an option as a career.

When I was around fifteen or sixteen, I saw another ad, this time for Volkswagen, where they claimed that a VW cost less per pound than hamburger, using a simple visual comparison. I thought this was genius on two counts: someone could conceptualize this as true because VWs are light and someone could do the math. There were some creative analytics going on there that intrigued me.

How do you define creativity?

I've always just marveled at creativity, regardless of the category or the subject matter. You can just kind of spot it when something's really new and not derivative. That poster behind us is beautiful and I appreciate it, but it's not particularly creative.

When you spot the purest form of creativity, it's something to behold. The band Phish is a good example. It's amazing the creativity of everything they do—even the purpose of the band. It's the same with Them Crooked Vultures. They're not just good bands. They have a level of creativity that's really pure and masterful. You can hear them for thirty seconds and get it.

Did you make a course correction early in your career?

Yes, in my sophomore year in college. I was an engineering major. I went to the program's Christmas party in the gym and found myself surrounded by a thousand of the geekiest men on the planet. They were mourning the death of the slide rule and expressing outrage over the advent

1) Become educated, dream about being an inventor. Leave home with #638

2) Make some $, ski, kix, seek a lifestyle.

3) 1st promotion, 1st time working with R.D. 1st taste for innovation.

4) Promoted again. Mentally ill CEO. 1year later senior mgt resigns.

5) 3.5 years of focused New products.

6) Big Company. Learned how to push ideas through a political environment.

7) The finish line! 25years of pure innovation. focus, great people, friends, start a family, lucky, inspiring environment. "HAPPY"

Steve's career map speaks for itself.

of the electronic calculator. There were no girls. No drinking. And this was their idea of a party. I knew right then I could not work with these people the rest of my life. I immediately transferred to marketing and I've never regretted it.

When did you first realize you could lead?

Very early. I was just comfortable with it. Now I lead like a producer or conductor. I'm confident pulling people together and directing them in different ways, but way before I had authority, I still could lead. I could sense that people around me wanted guidance and I was willing to offer it. Even people who were technically my superiors at work would be willing to let me lead them.

Over time my leadership style has adapted to whatever situation I'm in. Right now I need to micromanage more than I like because I have team members who need specific direction, but I don't like to do this.

Team sports are a good analogy, I think. How you play versus lead or coach is situational and depends on your team members. If you have really talented team members, you can focus more on being a player who leads and not so much a coach. If you have developing team members, you have to be more of a coach and mentor them. You have to spend less time playing and more time coaching. If you have weak players, you're just a coach—you have no time to be a player.

What do you love about your job?

Inventing—it's still what I love to do. For me, it's like going on a really awesome vacation with no reservations. You go to a really cool exotic place and you just start exploring.

Or maybe it's like fly fishing, which I also love. It takes all these years to learn the art and the science. There's all this cool equipment and technology and apps, but then there's also this combination of experience, motivation, and intuition or gut feeling. You bring these together and creating becomes a hunt. You're trying to catch this elusive "trout"—the big idea—in the river. You have to be patient and crafty. The little ones are easy to catch but not the big ones. They're big because they've never been caught. No one's figured them out yet.

Doing this is pure joy for me. It's so much fun. I never tire of looking at anything that stimulates my thinking, like observing behaviors or talking to others.

Do you think innovation depends more on process or people?

I think innovation is much more dependent on individual efforts and people. It's largely process independent. Not 100 percent—I don't know what the ratio is—but you have to have the right inventors. It's inventors, not the process of inventing. You have to be motivated to spend hours looking for insights and visuals—it takes a passion or drive that can't be captured in a process.

What's your "superpower" at work?

Patience. I know no one thinks of that as a superpower, but in my business, it is. As corny as it sounds, you can lead people (clients or employees) to water but you can't make them drink, even if they're dying of thirst. It takes true patience to wait until they're ready to change and then get a wide group of people to adopt that change.

What's helped you develop as a creative leader?

I'm a fine collaborator, but I'm a solitary thinker. The worst words I can hear in a group of people are, "Now we're going to break into teams of three." But I know it's important and I lead by example. When someone has a good idea, I explain why I think it was good. When they're off track, I help get them back on track in a way that doesn't bruise their ego. I don't want to do anything that will stifle creativity.

That's how people helped me. I seemed to always be surrounded by accidental support. People didn't know they were helping me, but they were. They encouraged me with balanced feedback and fair assessments. No one ever said, "You're a superstar" or "you're amazing." They would just calmly recognize when I did good work and let me know.

How important is corporate culture?

It's very important. What we sell is so intangible. People hire us and they hope their investment will result in a successful product. No one will invest in people or groups who aren't obviously and genuinely motivated and excited by what they do.

It's the same in reverse. We have relationships with people, not companies. That's what matters to us. When you find those right people and you connect with them, you get business relationships that are productive, creative, and successful.

But you can't mandate culture. I lead by example and I do my damnedest to firewall individuals and activities that damage the culture. What damages the culture? Bad attitudes, people who feel entitled, people who believe they have skills in excess of their demonstrated abilities, people who are unapproachable because they have a

quick temper or they're manipulative. These are bad traits in any culture, but they're really bad in a creative culture.

I also coach people never to fake it. If you don't know, just say, "I don't know, but I will find the answer for you." Occasionally I see people trying to fake it and it's so obvious and doesn't instill confidence. I have no trouble saying I don't know. I think it shows strength and people appreciate it.

Is your office design important to your creativity?

It's critical. Some big companies have labs with nice cabinets and everything is neat and tidy. We have no doors on anything. We took all the doors off our cabinets because we want to be able to see everything. Creativity is about iteration: you don't go from A to B. There's a lot of hard work iterating. We make that as easy as possible in our space. Nothing is behind a door. Imagine if your computer screen locked up every time you stopped typing—that's what a cabinet door is to us.

Our labs are very open. We work shoulder to shoulder. In the lab areas, shout mail is more important than email. Someone will yell out, "Does anyone have…?" I think it's under-appreciated how important proximity is to the creativity process. You don't want to be disruptive, but work environments find their own equilibrium over time.

How do you lead in a time of change?

The food industry evolves a little more slowly than other industries. The costs of change are very high. Change can happen fast at the entrepreneurial level or small restaurant level, where they can be more flexible and responsive. But everything on the menu here at Starbucks went through months of painful presentation and debate. The cost of building inventory is much more significant than with apps. If manufacturing is involved, it's very capital intensive. There's also little control over the retail environment. You have to hope it will sell. As a result, the industry is more risk averse and cautious.

But certain things like flavors can change really fast and I have to keep up with that. I read 93 blogs every day. I have an aggregator that creates a newspaper for me from all the blogs. The news is highly tailored to my professional needs. I also eat out a lot. Sometimes I try the same thing at different restaurants just to see how the style is developing. I've had moles in at least fifty different restaurants.

When it comes to the future, how do you know you're looking at the right things?

It's a result of experience, intuition, and your industry IQ (expertise). You can't have just one—you need all of them. You also have to be a risk taker. You have to be able to put a stake in the ground on an idea and have the confidence to defend it, even if others don't get it a first.

Have you made mistakes or had missed opportunities?

Sure, I make mistakes, but more than making mistakes I have certain weaknesses. I mean I don't land short of the runway—ever. But I'm overly sensitive to people's individual needs to the point that it gets in the way of progress at times. It probably goes hand in hand with patience, but this is not a virtue.

For example, because I understand how disruptive it is to let someone go, I may delay too long. But I feel such a sense of responsibility and I know this will disrupt their life, their self-esteem, their economic well-being. I could have a more profitable, smoother-running company if I was tougher on people issues, but I think of this as a speed bump. It's not going to do that much damage.

The upside of this is that because of my style and my slowness to take offense, employees come to me with bad news. They're not afraid I'll overreact. This lets me put out fires before they become roaring blazes. People with tempers have reputations. I want working relationships, not a reputation.

As for missed opportunities, my ideas get shot down all the time and always have. I've learned to accept it. Luckily, I've never been blocked from expressing my creative vision. Even if some of my ideas are crap, I'm still allowed to keep trying.

When you're gone from the scene, what three things do you want to be known for?

I could collaborate really well with people to create the very best possible outcome given the resources and constraints we were given. I was fun to work with, to the point that I made people happy. And that people would say of me, "Damn, he could come up with good ideas really fast." In my business, creative and fast are both important. Fast is probably slightly more important, because for my clients there's a competitive advantage to being first.

A DEO knows that nothing inhibits and undermines success more than the fear of failure. This dark-cloaked villain sneaks into offices in the guise of perfectionism or caution and stabs creativity in the chest. Given free rein, it can dominate an entire company, freezing it in time and killing its future.

Because of this, a DEO thinks differently about failure. He not only doesn't fear it, he gives it permission to happen regularly. Perhaps this is because he's realistic about its inevitability. But it's also because he recognizes failure as a key ingredient of success.

While we don't know of any central database of failures, John Kotter's seminal book *Leading Change* makes a convincing case that only 30 percent of companies' efforts to change result in success. That's a 70 percent fail rate and it's been repeatedly documented in different industries, departments, and specialties. Trying to avoid something that happens 70 percent of the time is a recipe for, well, another failure.

A DEO doesn't try to stop failure from happening because to him failure is learning. It's a test of current capabilities and strength of character. Failure is evidence of the courage to experiment

70% of companies' efforts to change fail.

Kotter, John. 1996. *Leading Change.* Boston: Harvard Business Review Press.

and take risks. To the DEO, failure is always at least partial success.

Unfortunately, most companies don't operate under this assumption. Companies headed by traditional CEOs often inadvertently create environments where failure is shameful and hidden.

Harvard Business School professor Amy Edmondson found a revealing dichotomy between what traditional executives believe about failure and how they act.[1] When she asked executives how many failures in their organizations were truly blameworthy, they estimated in the low single digits. When she asked how many failures were treated as blameworthy, the estimates rose to 70 percent or higher. As a consequence, she noted that many failures go unreported and their lessons are lost—meaning that someone else will inevitably repeat the failure.

Because a DEO doesn't fear failure, he creates a company that accommodates it and repurposes it. Because failure is not avoided, stakeholders recognize its normalcy. Leaders and employees create systems to report it and learn from it. In parallel, they emphasize their commitment to high-quality performance and notable achievements, communicating that what is truly shameful is to not learn from failure.

To help his company accept failure as a normal, functional aspect of business, a DEO introduces multiple ways to fail: forward, fast, harder, and publicly.

Fail forward

How is this done? A DEO starts by disconnecting failure from competence. Everyone, including a DEO, can fail. Reed Hastings, founder of Netflix, proved that in 2010 when he led his company to make some disastrous changes that immediately tanked its stock price and value. Reflecting on that move in an interview with CNBC, he said: "We learned a lot, that yes, you can be too slow, but you can also be too fast. And we just were too aggressive about going towards streaming." Instead of excuses or justifications, he offered a simple acknowledgment that he'd made a mistake and learned from it.

"

If you're not failing every now and again, it's a sign you're not doing anything very innovative.
Woody Allen

"

68%
of employee mistakes
go unreported to
management.

Edmondson, Amy. "Strategies for Learning from Failure." *Harvard Business Review.* April 2011.

A DEO highlights smart failures that help a company learn and course correct from stupid failures that repeat previous mistakes or ignore important facts. No DEOs reward clearly dumb failures. They waste time and resources, and they reinforce the notion that failure is bad. But failures that move the company forward through what they teach or train are smart.

Fail harder

A common reaction to the fear of failure is to hesitate or proceed cautiously, ever on the alert for warning signs. But this hedging against failure has the unfortunate side effect of making failure more likely. By not fully committing to our ambitions, we communicate our doubts to others. We let the future know we aren't ready for it.

The phrase, "fail harder," reminds a DEO and his team to proceed with enthusiasm and complete devotion to their ambitions. It cautions him to avoid riding the breaks too much as he picks up speed. It also reminds him that failure is likely despite his wholehearted efforts. To fail harder does not mean to ignore feedback, take

foolish risks, or abandon all cautions. Instead, it counsels the DEO and his team to pursue only those visions that capture them totally.

Fail fast

Another tactic a DEO uses is to define success clearly and in small bits. This not only makes it easier for colleagues and clients to collaborate, but also helps them keep failures minimal and identify them quickly. John Bielenberg, founder of Future Partners, encourages making small bets with communities who depend on the change being tested. These communities are more likely to assess the small bet accurately and to provide useful feedback.

The tricks of Silicon Valley rely heavily on fast failure. Beta versions are released with the expectation that they contain "bugs" or mistakes. Pivots—fast course corrections—are part of any realistic project plan. A failed startup is not the end of an entrepreneur's career; in fact, it may lead directly to his next success.

Fail publicly

To learn from failure a DEO pushes for transparency and shared accountability. Transparency makes it easier to identify failures quickly. Shared accountability ensures that everything is a team effort, so there's no such thing as individual failure. When a team fails at something, a DEO looks for solutions in the system, not in the people.

Finally, a DEO works to create an environment where feedback is accepted as guidance, not judgment. Honest feedback is sometimes difficult to receive, so a DEO role models it by soliciting and paying close attention to feedback on his own performance. He may not like it, but he does it.

1 Edmondson, Amy. "Strategies for Learning from Failure." *Harvard Business Review.* April 2011. http://hbr.org/2011/04/strategies-for-learning-from-failure/ar/

Workouts to increase your permission to fail

Stretch it.

Define and set small goals that are just outside your comfort zone—reachable but requiring effort. Break the goals into even smaller parts until each seems doable. Reward yourself for trying to reach each goal, whether you succeed or fail.

"SFD."

Adopt an attitude that lets first iterations show up in any form. In writing this book, Maria pushed for "shitty first drafts," which took considerable pressure off the team working on it and allowed us to express our ideas more freely.

Be vulnerable.

Learn the power of being more vulnerable. Brené Brown, a research professor at the University of Houston Graduate College of Social Work, makes a convincing argument that being vulnerable is not a weakness, but rather the most accurate measure of courage. When you accept failure as inevitable, it no longer controls you. If this feels too uncomfortable, keep the results to yourself at first until its seems more natural. Watch her extraordinary TED video, "The Power of Vulnerability."

Fail smiling.

Fail on purpose. Choose an objective you have little chance of achieving but continue working at it. Take up ballet at forty or try to make the team in a sport you've just learned. Bowl blindfolded. Swim against a current. The point is not only to persevere despite success, but also to enjoy what failing can teach you.

GO DEEPER
Being Wrong: Adventures in the Margin of Error by Kathryn Schulz
Better by Mistake: The Unexpected Benefits of Being Wrong by Alina Tugend
The Power of Vulnerability: Teachings on Authenticity, Connection, and Courage by Brené Brown
Brilliant Mistakes: Finding Success on the Far Side of Failure by Paul J. H. Schoemaker
The Wisdom of Failure by Laurence G. Weinzimmer and Jim McConoughey

Play is dismissed far too easily in the workplace. It's not forbidden anymore, but traditional leaders consider it recreation, a reprieve from normal effort. Thankfully, even the most serious-minded DEO recognizes the folly in ignoring play.

In most workplaces, play is a break meant to refresh or reward employees who then return to their real focus—work. Even in this carefully moderated role play is suspect. A company that spends too much on a retreat or hires an entertaining trainer will attract critics who question the legitimacy of these "nonproductive" expenses.

But academics and developmental scientists have studied play for generations and confirmed its worth in nearly every aspect of human life, including at work. A DEO doesn't need to second-guess these experts. He puts play to work building a cohesive culture, developing better solutions, and generating more creative ideas. To a DEO, separating play from work is foolish.

Certainly play is pleasurable and relaxing—the perfect antidote to stress. But beyond stress reduction, playing and laughing can transport people to a more creative state of mind.[1] It can loosen inhibitions and get synapses firing. More importantly, it can turn off the more judgmental part of our brains. With the judgment filter off, ideas flow more freely.

Play contributes to social, emotional, and cognitive development.[2] It not only makes us smarter, we are smarter when we're playing, particularly if a goal or some level of competition is introduced. For example, Foldit, a computer game, presents gamers with levels of puzzles—all of which are based on the folding of protein strands. This may not sound as much fun as a rousing game of *Cards Against Humanity,* but over 240,000 people find it highly entertaining. Their play redesigned a protein and helped decipher the structure of a virus that had eluded conventional research for 15 years.[3]

Play also allows the practice and development of skills without the pressure of evaluation or set expectations. "Playacting" can prepare people for issues they may encounter under more demanding or constrained situations. Pretending to be someone else—like a client or a customer—improves empathy and can deliver particularly resonant insights. Bodystorming (playacting as if a product or service exists) can uncover problems or potentials at an early development stage when revisions are still possible.

In addition to its generative powers, play lowers defenses and makes people more receptive. It can connect groups in a way that meetings or other activities rarely can. It often opens new channels of communication, for example, between different departments or different levels of the organization, by showing our more humane or interesting side.

Given the benefits of play it's a wonder that any company ever considers work a preferred activity, but fun can't be forced. Installing a company slide or condoning crazy business card titles won't make a company playful. To get serious about play, a DEO integrates it into the company's environment and processes.

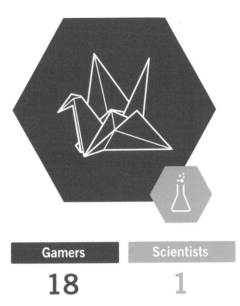

Gamers	Scientists
18	1

Gamers "playing" in a Foldit contest reengineered an enzyme to increase its activity by more than 18 times compared to earlier work by scientists.

Marshall, Jessica. 2012. "Victory for crowdsourced biomolecule design." *Nature.* http://www.nature.com/news/victory-for-crowdsourced-biomolecule-design-1.9872]

Playful environments

Playful environments start with toys. Toys are the viruses of play. Balls, puzzle pieces, Legos, stuffed animals, water pistols—all are designed to infect us with the desire to play. Pick one up and we become contagious, quickly spreading the bug to others. With toys in hand, the only defense against the affliction of play is a sour attitude or a packed schedule.

For this reason, DEOs welcome toys in the office. Some even build playrooms. They happily litter the environment with large inflatable balls, mind puzzles, Nerf darts, and other harmless provocations of play. If all these playthings do is lighten

Rather than declaring a "play day" or keeping play separate from work, DEOs integrate it in their companies' daily activities.

the mood, that's enough. If they help harried clients unwind and think more broadly, that's a win. If they spur a breakthrough idea, that's the bonus round.

Playful processes

Rather than declaring a "play day" or keeping play separate from work, DEOs integrate it into their companies' daily activities. Silicon Valley companies are notorious for finding ways to combine work and play. For example, Google is famous for its "20 percent time," an unofficial program that allows engineers to spend roughly eight hours a week working on whatever they want. This freedom to play not only attracts talent, but also encourages exploration of intriguing spaces that might otherwise go unnoticed.

A DEO might create contests to get coworkers' competitive juices up or prompt higher sales.

He might schedule a planning meeting on the ski slopes or a strategy session at the zoo. Despite their high recreational factor, these are not boondoggles. Integrating play into normal work activities extends enthusiasm and energy. It also has a reputation for preceding significant eureka moments.

A DEO integrates play into the workday by embracing and modeling it. He relishes pranks and practical jokes. He laughs easily. He admires the mischievous clerk and the perpetually happy lab technician. He welcomes play to work each day, hoping it won't leave early.

1 Johnson, James E. May 30–31, 2007. "Play and Creativity." (Prepared for the Play and Creativity Conference, Tainan, R.O.C.)
2 Brown, Stuart L. 2009. *Play: How It Shapes the Brain, Opens the Imagination, and Invigorates the Soul.* New York: Avery.
3 Marshall, Jessica. 2012. "Victory for Crowdsourced Biomolecule Design." *Nature,* January 22. doi:10.1038/nature.2012.9872.

Workouts to improve your playfulness

Play ball.

If your company doesn't integrate play into its normal work processes, lead the change with "baby steps." Start a softball or soccer team. Create a "game night" where employees can challenge one another to an ongoing series of games. If you meet resistance, try bowling or miniature golf.

Join the masses.

Join the hundreds of millions of people worldwide who enjoy massive multiplayer online games that immerse them in social role-playing through the use of avatars. Or join a community like Solve It for Science where participants solve scientific problems through play.

Start something.

Bring toys into your next meeting. Leave them in the center of the table and wait patiently. Eventually someone will start playing and soon everyone will join in. Need inspiration? There are online stores that specialize in office toys. Visit them.

Make play dates.

Initiate departmental or company outings. Attend a baseball game or a concert as a group. Try kayaking or hiking en masse. See a popular movie on its release date. If your group is large enough, take over the theatre.

Start over.

If you've gone years without playing, start over with the basics. Visit a playground on the weekend and try out the swings. Graduate to a scooter and race around your block. Play Monopoly with a ten-year-old, ideally in a treehouse. If even the thought of these activities makes you squirm, do more of them.

GO DEEPER

Play: How It Shapes the Brain, Opens the Imagination, and Invigorates the Soul by Stuart Brown
Homo Ludens: A Study of the Play-Element in Culture by Johan Huizinga
Creative Intelligence: Harnessing the Power to Create, Connect, and Inspire by Bruce Nussbaum

ITERATE AND EVOLVE

Our ingrained image of evolution is a smooth transition that starts with ape and leads to man. But this is the executive summary of evolution. The details include countless iterations which over time shaped who we are today. DEOs embrace the same iterative process to evolve their businesses.

For a DEO, change is constant and reinventing her organization is the norm, not the exception. Innovation is not caged in a lab and focused solely on new products or services, but spreads freely through the building, infusing all aspects of the company.

Like any evolving organism, the company senses and responds to its environment, developing new strengths and capabilities as needed. Processes are continually modified to suit emerging needs. Positions, and the people who hold them, shift regularly as well. If a new project calls for strong people skills, an HR executive may head it. If the project requires a detail orientation, a statistician may find himself in charge.

Some find this state of flux too chaotic. Traditional CEOs might regard it as a breakdown of order, a problem that needs to be fixed.

But a DEO feels that it's healthy and natural. She knows that constant iteration builds agility and nimbleness, two traits that her market demands and rewards. She knows that it pushes people to hone their skills, adopt a more progressive mindset, and embrace course correction as part of their routine.

The development benefits of an iterative approach to innovation, both as a practice and a process, are almost too numerous to list. Regular course corrections encourage feedback and extract real insights from stakeholders. Misunderstandings and confusion are quickly identified and addressed. Modular workloads are easier to balance and allocate among teams. Costs are easier to assess. Systems are easier to update. Learnings are recycled faster and more frequently. Finally, and perhaps ironically, risks are reduced.[1]

Giant companies like Amazon, Apple, Facebook, and Google have practiced continual design iteration for much of their relatively young lives. Startups following Eric Ries's recommendations in *The Lean Startup* have learned to create "minimum viable products" (MVPs) as a way of testing and then iterating a company concept with the least investment of time, effort, and money.[2] As a recent example, the Obama 2012 presidential campaign repeatedly tweaked and tested their community outreach software, gathering feedback from users in the field. In contrast, the Romney campaign developed and deployed their software without iteration or real-world testing. On Election Day, the Obama system performed admirably; the Romney system crashed and burned.[3]

Despite its many benefits, an evolutionary process can produce hazards. Arbitrary disruption that happens with no direction is just as harmful to a company as enforced complacency. Multiple modules and versions scattered across departments without a plan for assembly are as deadly to a project as rigid models. To pilot a company through the rapids of iteration, a DEO needs a cohesive crew and a strong navigational instinct.

Design iterations

The majority of designs go through four or five major design iterations.

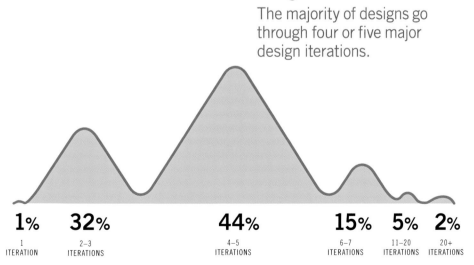

1%	32%	44%	15%	5%	2%
1 ITERATION	2–3 ITERATIONS	4–5 ITERATIONS	6–7 ITERATIONS	11–20 ITERATIONS	20+ ITERATIONS

Aberdeen Group. Jun 2006. "Managing Product Relationships: Enabling Iteration and Innovation in Design."

Engage others

When there are no five-year business plans and no cast-in-concrete operation manuals, much depends on personal relationships. A DEO's colleagues trust her to make spontaneous decisions. She balances her desire to push toward the future with the recognition that her credibility is at risk. No one expects perfection, but candor, openness, and accountability are basic equipment for the journey.

A DEO talks openly about the importance of iterations and takes personal charge of communicating it to the company. She realizes that change must be socialized rather than mandated. She communicates the company's general path forward, while remaining open to stakeholders' concerns and contributions. She understands that everyone in the company—and all the company's clients, partners, and customers—are on the ride together.

Look ahead

We don't need to search historical files to learn the fate of businesses that didn't peer far enough ahead. Kodak, which dominated photography little more than a decade ago, misjudged the rough waters of digital imagery. Blockbuster, long the king of video rentals, miscalculated the impact of streaming video. Hostess Brands, whose cupcakes filled millions of lunchboxes, thought the healthy food trend wouldn't sink them.

To avoid this fate, the DEO uses the business equivalent of high-powered binoculars: trend reports, detail-rich ethnographic research, and contemplative strategy sessions. These undercurrents of insight help a DEO envision a future that is not a linear progression from today. They prompt her and those around her to ask what if and what can be. They force the company to look in new directions.

Stay flexible but firm

The choppiness of constant change and reinvention is more tolerable when a company has explicit and deeply felt core values that serve as rudders. The path may vary from day to day, but the organization traveling it stays consistent in what it seeks and values.

This is not to say that visions and values remain unchanged in the hands of a DEO. They too may evolve, but much more slowly and with great deliberation. Changing company values is not an iteration—it's a new journey.

Make smart moves

Smart iterations require continual learning, constant generation of new knowledge, regular sharing, and perpetual revisions. This translates into ceaseless research to understand how customers are changing. It means having regular brainstorming sessions to keep a flow of new ideas coming. It means rapid prototyping of concepts and beta testing as a standard practice.

It also means a steady stream of real-time data. Accounting reports that provide an overview of the past month or quarter may be useful for slow-moving decisions, but their value pales in comparison to daily or even hourly injections of click rates, likes, visits, and purchases.

---

1 Murphy, Cliff. "Reducing Risk and Increasing the Probability of Project Success." http://www.projectsmart.co.uk/reducing-risk-increasing-probability-of-project-success.html

2 Ries, Eric. 2011. *The Lean Startup: How Today's Entrepreneurs Use Continuous Innovation to Create Radically Successful Businesses*. New York: Crown Business.

3 Kolakowski, Nick. January 9, 2013. "The Billion-Dollar Startup: Inside Obama's Campaign Tech." Slashdot. http://slashdot.org/topic/bi/the-billion-dollar-startup-inside-obamas-campaign-tech/

Workouts to help you learn to iterate and evolve

Do it over.

The next time you need to write a report or complete a task, approach it through a series of revisions. Do a rough draft or "comp" without regard for details. Let someone else review it (acknowledging that it's only an early draft). Incorporate their feedback and do a second draft. Repeat this process until you've completed the assignment or your colleague starts avoiding you—whichever comes first. Look back over all the drafts and notice how the piece evolved.

Check progress.

Ask to see early versions of work you admire. Whether it's art, music, literature, or an annual report, looking back at early stages of development can provide an interesting view of how iteration fuels and influences creativity.

Pass it on.

Start a drawing or a story and ask someone else to add to it. Continue passing the item around, letting others direct its evolution. When it's complete, post it where it can remind you that letting go doesn't mean dropping the ball.

Throw it out.

Learn to delete. Throwing out that which we no longer need is part of evolving. Edit your work style, your perspectives, your relationships, your ideas. Look keenly at your favorite behaviors or beliefs to make sure they haven't become outdated or obsolete. Have the courage to end expensive blunders before they become catastrophic mistakes.

GO DEEPER

Organizations Evolving by Howard Aldrich and Martin Ruef
Dealing with Darwin by Geoffrey A. Moore
The Lean Startup by Eric Ries
The Science of Serendipity: How to Unlock the Promise of Innovation by Matt Kingdon

Chris Anderson

Curator for TED Conferences

Chris Anderson could easily hide in a crowd. His quiet demeanor seems more suited to a chemist or minister than the curator of TED, the wildly successful nonprofit media phenomenon devoted to "ideas worth spreading."

We interviewed Anderson in his New York office, where modern furnishings and warm hardwood floors coexist comfortably. With the sounds of the city in the background, he described a career that only a DEO could have designed.

As a child, what did you think you'd be when you grew up?

I wanted to be a vet. My dad was a doctor. I wanted to be different and I loved my dog. That was about the logic. It didn't last long though, and I kind of resigned myself to my fate and agreed that I'd be a doctor. Helping people seemed more useful long-term than helping animals.

Happily, when I was about 18, I had this exhilarating moment of clarity where I understood that I'd make a truly terrible doctor. I couldn't remember all the detail needed and had no patience for patients. I was excited by biology, but the thought of training for three or four years and then dealing endlessly with individuals was actually quite, quite stressful.

Mass media seemed exciting, possibly because I'm an introvert and it meant less connecting with people one-on-one. The notion of journalism, of writing words once and—if they were good—having them seen by potentially millions of people through the magic of the printing press, was exciting. I've always been on this edge between loving language and loving science, and not really finding many careers that embrace both in an interesting way.

Home computers came on the market in the UK in about 1981, which is when I bought one and was completely hooked. I discovered my inner geek, which frankly never really went away. I did a few different journalism things at the start, but

when the opportunity came to be an editor of a computer magazine, that was wildly exciting. I did that for a year and then leapt to the entrepreneurial side.

Was your move from editor to entrepreneur intentional or accidental?

It wasn't originally intentional. There was no business in my family at all. The thought of being an entrepreneur had never crossed my mind. What attracted me was doing the job and seeing that it was suddenly becoming possible to make magazines on a much smaller scale. It was possible to print from computer-typeset copy, so suddenly three kids with a home computer could actually design a magazine and get it printed.

That's how it started. I left my last magazine job as an employee, and three months later we had a magazine on sale in the UK. It still kind of amazes me that that happened. There was no Internet. There was just an explosion of interest in all manner of niche topics, especially around computers. We had the wild experience of a business that made money in its first year and then doubled in scale, in employees, and in profitability, every year for seven years after that. We had that wonderful experience of getting together a critical mass of amazing people who want to work for each other and who attract other great people.

What was most important to you at that time?

As a small company, we were obsessed with the idea of passion. The company's slogan was "media with passion" and the idea was to be this rebel army taking on the big publishers. Our secret weapon was to know much more deeply and viscerally what readers actually wanted because we were the readers. We didn't employ traditional journalists, per se. We employed people who were passionate about the topics, like computer geeks and video game aficionados. We taught them how to share their passion. The place was humming with that kind of excitement.

On one hand, it was the excitement of being the outsiders, taking on much, much bigger companies who had many more resources. We had the fire that all those readers connected to, and we had a couple of ideas that other people hadn't thought of, like selling a magazine plus software packages. For us, it was completely obvious why readers would pay double the price for that package than they would for a traditional magazine. But it didn't seem obvious to the other publishers for a surprisingly long time.

What was the first moment that you considered yourself to be a leader?

The moment of realization was a year after we had started, when we launched a second magazine that was successful. Seeing the reader response to that second magazine was a "holy cow" moment—I thought, "This is actually going to work, and by the way, there are going to be lots more magazines after this one." So it felt like a passion at that point. It was wildly, mind-blowingly exciting because I had no idea that was going to be possible.

What was your leadership style?

I certainly didn't lead with a command and control style. I try to lead through the power of enthusiasm. You know, the best idea wins.

TED

Dot-com Crash

Biz career takes off

Chris plays with his future until it snaps into a career of shared discovery and positive passion.

I'll say, "Guys, guys, guys, we could launch this!" or "This would be amazing, and here's why!" or "If you did it this way, and this way, people would love that, they'd love it!"

Often those ideas would be barking mad, and I'd get pushback or they would fail. But the place was absolutely brimming with launch ideas. We launched, launched, launched. In that first seven years, we launched 32 successful magazines—I think we launched about 40 total, and I think about eight failed. Thirty-two made it and stayed profitable. It was just a thrilling culture to be part of. It was very much "go for it" and "try it."

What are your strengths at work?

I let the power of the idea be the spark. I don't think it's me on a personal or social interaction level. Almost everyone in the world could do a better job than me. But at the level of "Here's a really great idea and here's why it's great," I can get people excited.

There's often a moment when an idea snaps into place. Several words fit here: adventure, design, imagination. It's the human skill of being able to play with the future, and model it and rapidly iterate lots and lots of different combinations in your mind until one snaps into place, and for whatever reason, you say, "This is it. "

One of the benefits of being an introvert, or at least being inward-looking, is that you spend more time in that place, in your inner world playing with the future. I'm very future oriented. I've always been someone who looks forward rather than back, and when something feels right about the future, it feels very right. Typically that comes from pulling together ideas from several different sources. These different things sort of play around and some don't feel right. Then suddenly something can feel very, very right and it sort of snaps.

> "
> # I certainly didn't lead with a command and control style. I try to lead through the power of enthusiasm.
> "

You wake up at three o'clock in the morning wild with excitement. You go and explain it to people and even though you explain to them stuttering and in a very non-charismatic way, you do it with passion and excitement, so the idea wins. People go, "Oh, that really would work, that's cool," and then a critical mass of people gets excited and you can make it happen.

How do you sustain that kind of creativity?

The more you open yourself up to unexpected sources of stimulation, the more likely you are to have that big moment. Steve Jobs, you know, credited a lot of his success to a course in calligraphy at Reed College.

Certainly some of the best TED moments are when you hear something and think there's no way this person could be interesting and then—zing!—it really connects with you. I had

> **Embrace the chaos and just realize that we're in a time when an element of letting go can be unbelievably powerful.**

that experience a couple of years ago watching a dance troupe perform and hearing these guys say, "Yeah, dance is morphing now. Kids are learning from each other across the other side of the world courtesy of YouTube." I thought, "Holy cow, that's exactly what's happening with TED speakers." People are learning from each other. This insight came from a completely ridiculous source. You've got to put a lot of ingredients into the pot before you stir it up.

Is there a process you follow?

I would say that it happens more by bringing together creative people. When we gave away the talks, June Cohen was very much involved with that and there were external people who suggested that we try some stuff online. It

started out as an experiment. The big aha came when I saw the intensity of people's reactions to those first six talks online. When people responded passionately, we got really excited. And so on the basis of their emails, we sort of flipped TED from being just a conference to anchoring it around the website.

If you were a traditional control-oriented person who wanted everything to be measured and known and risk free, you just wouldn't do this. It's not worth the stress. So, the core of what you have to do, in a sense, is embrace the chaos and just realize that we're in a time when an element of letting go can be unbelievably powerful. You let go in order to get back. There's the occasional embarrassment here or there, but you embrace it.

Ladies and gentlemen, if you want a Wikipedia that's error free, you won't have Wikipedia. Embrace it and move on. I mean, yes, have rules; make them as public as possible. Enlist the community to help enforce them and keep iterating. People don't need to be told what they can't do; they need to be shown how to be great. We help people understand how to do a great job creating and how to do a great job coaching speakers. We pass on knowledge as fast as we can and allow people to learn from each other as well.

Have you had any failures?

The whole TEDx experiment was born out of failure, or a form of failure. We had Pangea Day that involved people around the world gathering to watch films at the same time. It was a fantastic event. It was beautiful in many ways, but financially, it was a painful failure. We didn't get enough sponsors and it was incredibly expensive. But one of the things that wasn't expensive and was successful was this

The extraordinary team of collaborators who work together to create the TED experience.

self-organized program of allowing people to create their own little gatherings. Fifteen hundred people did that.

Paying attention to that made us think we could tap into the TED experience at a grassroots level, but that would involve giving away the brand, which we couldn't do. So we pulled people together and we brainstormed. There was a moment when the idea snapped and we came up with TEDx. It felt close enough to TED that people would die to do these events, but distant enough that we could say these are self-organized. That just felt right and it felt very clear that we had to try it.

What three things do you want to be known for?

I would like to be known as the person who didn't retire. You can stay engaged in the world of ideas until you die. And when you can't, you should die. I would like to be thought of as generous. In the connected world, you can argue it's the smart thing to do because a lot of things can get passed around very, very quickly. Generosity tends to be its own reward. It's infectious and I think it's been core to TED's success. Every time we've given stuff away, it's benefited us. Finally, I'd like to be known as a dreamer, as a guy obsessed with ideas.

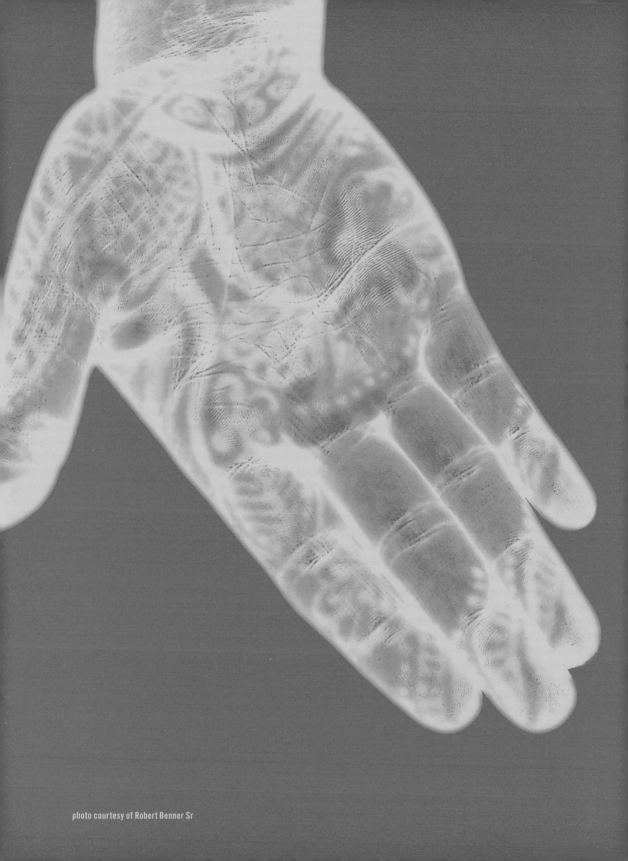
photo courtesy of Robert Benner Sr

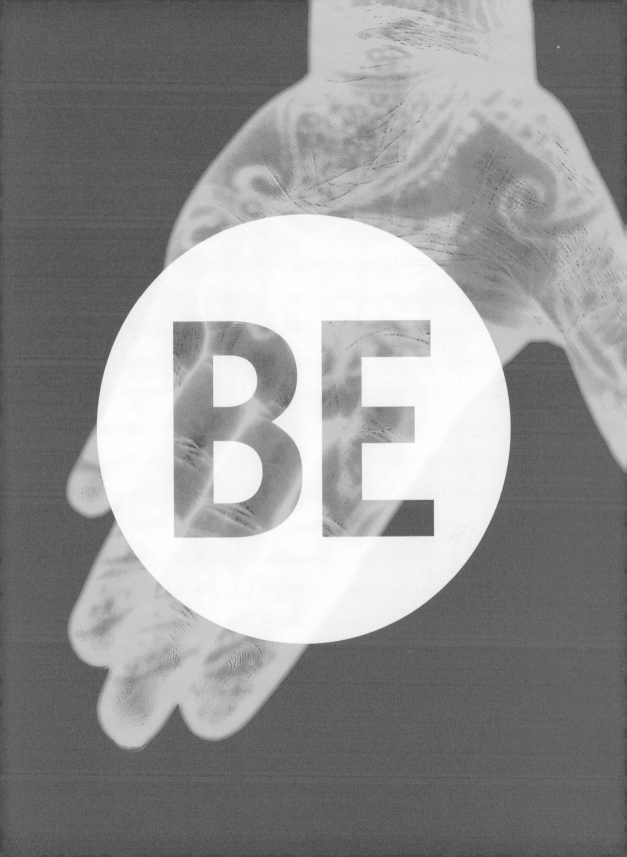

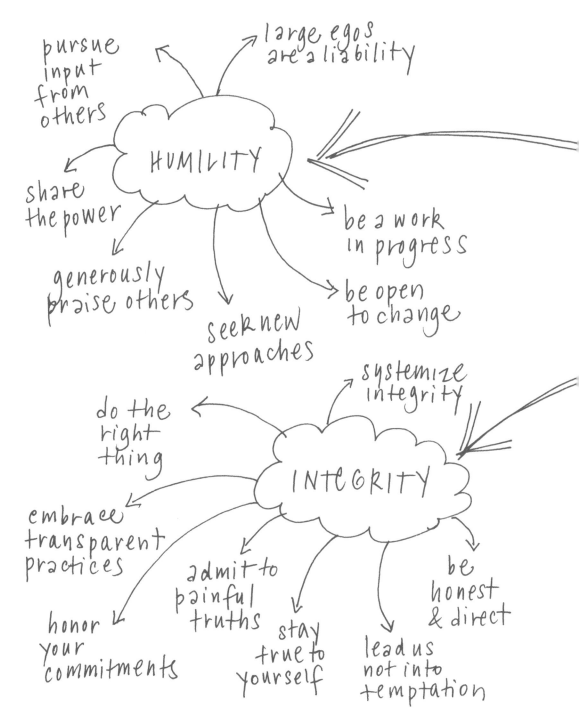

pursue input from others

large egos are a liability

HUMILITY

share the power

be a work in progress

generously praise others

seek new approaches

be open to change

systemize integrity

do the right thing

INTEGRITY

embrace transparent practices

admit to painful truths

stay true to yourself

be honest & direct

honor your commitments

lead us not into temptation

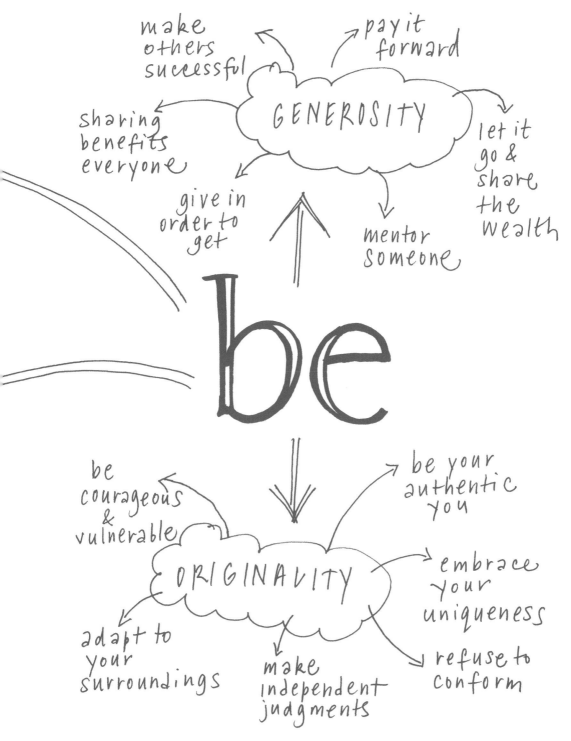

make others successful

pay it forward

GENEROSITY

sharing benefits everyone

let it go & share the wealth

give in order to get

mentor someone

be

be courageous & vulnerable

be your authentic you

ORIGINALITY

embrace your uniqueness

adapt to your surroundings

make independent judgments

refuse to conform

153

Such a simple word. Such a rich, multifaceted meaning. Having integrity means adhering to the values, beliefs, and principles we claim to hold. It means doing the right thing no matter the consequences. It may mean incurring a loss in order to honor our commitments. It means never saying that the ends justify the means.

A DEO with integrity aligns his personal and business values in a way that is honest, reasonable, and authentic. A vegan DEO may agree to employee meat-eaters, but his client list won't include the National Cattlemen's Foundation. A pacifist DEO will not try to rationalize working with the Department of Defense.

A DEO with integrity makes his values clear to others. He maintains candid and open communications with stakeholders about the company's goals and the path it is taking to reach those goals. He doesn't publicly post every stray idea that pops into his head, but he does speak willingly about the company's processes and

Perceived Authenticity

Customers' perception of a company's authenticity is made up of three parts: products and services, management behaviors, and societal impact.

FleishmanHillard. 2012. Authenticity Gap: Managing Expectations and Experience.

MANAGEMENT BEHAVIOR

SOCIETAL IMPACT

30% 25%

45%

CUSTOMER BENEFITS

decisions. A DEO with integrity admits to painful truths, rather than asserting a "wide stance."

A DEO sets his standard for integrity high and encourages those he works with to do the same, but this ambition may come at a cost. Integrity is often in conflict with profitability, especially in the short-term. To honor his values or commitments, a DEO may have to ignore a hot trend. He may have to avoid doing business in a country with a billion potential customers. He may need to say no thanks to a major client. He may have to operate at a loss until a market large enough to sustain his company shares his vision.

It's difficult to discuss integrity without invoking its partner virtue, authenticity. When a DEO prizes integrity, he has no choice but to endorse authenticity and to follow the famous maxim: "to thine own self be true." Authenticity, whether at a personal level, brand level, or company level, means a match between the face we show to others and the truth of who we are. Unfortunately, while most leaders extol authenticity, few companies produce it.

A recent FleishmanHillard study measured what it called the "Authenticity Gap,"[1] the gap between what customers expect from a company or industry and what they actually experience. Because customers increasingly expect to be in

a relationship with the brands they buy, they likewise expect the companies to honestly deliver on their promises and commitments, not just in terms of product satisfaction, but also in terms of management behavior and community impact.

When a company is inauthentic—when it promises more than it can deliver—it erodes these relationships, and no amount of customer service or deep discounts can patch them. On the other hand, when no gap exists between a company's values and its behavior—when it's authentic and operates with integrity—customers turn into advocates, selling the brand to their friends, their family, and even complete strangers.

DEOs would value integrity and authenticity even if they were a sunk cost, but thankfully that's not the case. A company that respects and rewards these values not only pleases more customers, but also operates more smoothly.[2] Vision and values are integrated into daily activities and become stronger guides of everyone's behavior. Those who disagree with the company's goals aren't encouraged to hide their beliefs; instead, they're encouraged to leave. Trust spreads, making it easier to implement decisions and delegate responsibility.

A DEO develops integrity in his organization by building it into the company's operating systems. He maintains it by recognizing

"

Real integrity is doing the right thing, knowing that nobody's going to know whether you did it or not.
Oprah Winfrey

"

the ongoing challenge presented by constant change and diligently assessing the integrity of his own and his company's decisions.

Systemizing integrity

Ensuring integrity in an organization takes a DEO's time and effort. Consultants can't invent it and it can't be faked for long. A good starting point is the company's vision and values. If they don't accurately reflect what the company does and what the DEO believes, they'll do more harm than good and should be revised. If a company's vision and values are trendy, if they could be found on a "most popular corporate visions" list, odds are they don't match the company's actions. If a company's vision and values are vague, they may generally match its actions, but not in a way that differentiates them.

Embracing transparent practices is a good next step. DEOs have varying appetites for transparency, and there are some good arguments for why some information deserves to be kept private. But to the extent possible, employees should know and respect a company's decision-making

process. This includes a clear understanding of leadership roles and responsibilities, as well as an unhindered view of how the company makes its profit and what impact its production process has on communities and the planet.

Transparency is achieved through honesty and directness. A DEO inspires company-wide candor by communicating all outcomes: wins, losses, awards, and mistakes. When a DEO reverses a previous position or adopts a new position that is seemingly in conflict with the company's values, he acknowledges the discrepancy and explains the rational.

Maintaining integrity

Maintaining integrity can be as challenging as building it. A DEO faces daily temptations to lower costs, avoid taxes, reduce staffing, ignore environmental damage, and a host of other negative actions that bring positive bottom-line benefits. When competitors take these actions and aren't penalized, the pressure grows even more intense. Yet this is the ultimate test of integrity: doing the right thing when it's not easy.

A DEO struggles with temptations as we all do, but he accepts and plans for these pressures, recognizing little dishonesties or inauthentic behavior as a shortcut to a cliff. He urges those around him to act as guards, alerting decision makers when a company's integrity is in jeopardy.

A DEO also plans for his company's values to evolve. He encourages stakeholders to help with that evolution through co-creation of new products and services, through public commentary, and through ongoing dialogue. A DEO knows his company can't stand still or freeze its vision and values in time. But if everyone understands the company's core essence, new versions can emerge with the same authenticity as the original.

---

1 The Authenticity Gap, 2012, FleishmanHillard.
2 Covey, Stephen M. R. 2011. *The Speed of Trust.* New York: Free Press.

Workouts to improve your integrity

Know thyself.

Integrity starts with self-awareness. Gaining self-awareness is critical to integrity and authenticity; after all, it's tough to be true to yourself if you're unsure of who you are. In part this awareness comes with time, but therapy, coaching, training, or even self-help books may speed the process.

Be known.

If you know yourself relatively well, find out if others see you in the same way. If you're a shy geek at heart, but you act like Louis CK around your colleagues, is it you they like or the person you're imitating? If your true self is an unruly artist, but you're a quiet analyst in the office, which person is in charge? The pressure to integrate your public and private selves into a cohesive whole has increased with the advent of social networks. Don't share what you prefer to keep private, but do let others have a peek at your nonprofessional life. If they're surprised, try for better integration.

Commit.

Keep track of commitments. This seems trivial, but listing what you've agreed to do not only serves as a reminder, but also helps limit what you offer. As your list grows, you'll be more aware of your current obligations and less likely to take on new ones.

Find the good.

Avoid those who don't value integrity. Diversity is usually beneficial, but spending time with people who don't have integrity makes sense only if you have a martyr complex or are a corrections officer. If neither of those descriptions applies, find new colleagues.

GO DEEPER

Integrity: The Courage to Meet the Demands of Reality by Dr. Henry Cloud
The Integrity Dividend: Leading by the Power of Your Word by Tony Simons
Honest Business by Michael Phillips and Salli Rasberry
True North: Discover Your Authentic Leadership by Bill George and Peter Sims
All Marketers Are Liars by Seth Godin

HUMILITY

Perhaps the easiest way to explain humility is to say that it's the opposite of arrogance. Where arrogance is an exaggerated sense of superiority and dominance, humility is an acknowledgment of limitations and connectedness. Humility may not be an ingrained trait of all DEOs, but it is an ideal they all seek.

Where arrogance arises from a focus on the self, humility comes from connecting with a higher ideal—a mission or goal that makes the self less important. Jim Collins's classic work, *Good to Great*, heralded the importance of humility when he identified it as an essential trait of high-performing leaders. But the message bears repeating, particularly to a generation raised on the brash, self-serving antics of leveraged buyout bunglers, narcissistic bloggers, and scene-stealing politicians. Leaders don't need outsized egos to command respect and inspire others. In fact, in an era of constant change and disruptive innovation, large egos are a liability.

DEOs recognize and value humility in themselves and their coworkers. They understand it's based in a sense of worthiness and a pride that is "right-sized." It's confidence that is quiet. It's passion that is purposeful.

That's not to say that humility hangs out with meekness. To the contrary, meekness suggests resignation and submission. No DEO finds solace in those behaviors. Humility does, however, accept the possibility of "error blindness," a term Kathryn Schulz explains in her book, *Being Wrong*. Error blindness is the human tendency to not see where we may be at fault.

Like most of us, a DEO wants to believe that she's right, but she's trained herself over time to accept the possibility that she's not. By recognizing the possibility that she can be wrong, a DEO is more likely to have accurate and perceptive self-awareness. She'll monitor her behavior more closely, looking for signs of bias or a rush to judgment. She'll worry anytime she hears someone say, "This is how we've always done it." She'll stay up nights debating whether her latest decision was brilliant or boneheaded.

Interestingly, a DEO's humility strengthens her ability to generously praise others. Certainly this can win her more friends, but it has a practical side as well. By sharing credit with her contributors and expressing confidence in their abilities, she improves cooperation, relationships, and a sense of fairness. By accepting responsibility when results are poor and fixing problems rather than assigning blame, she builds a culture of commitment, creativity, and support.

Work in progress

A DEO's acceptance of fallibility frees her from the false need for perfection and instead encourages her to continually improve. She knows she doesn't have to excel at everything. She can be a work in progress and those around her can enjoy similar freedom.

A commitment to continual improvement signals openness to feedback and openness to change. For a DEO, this is not a passive posture. She actively pursues input from others and expects them to welcome it from her. She reaches out to experts, customers, vendors, partners, and anyone else who might have a novel or insightful angle. She encourages participation across disciplines and departments, seeking new perspectives and different approaches. She serves the members of her community potent ingredients—transformative information, fresh experiences, and data that sings—and then works with them to create the next "aha!" moment.

> "
> # Humility is not thinking less of yourself, it's thinking of yourself less.
> ## C. S. Lewis
> "

She reaches out to experts, customers, vendors, partners, and anyone else who might have a novel or insightful angle on how she can improve. By being receptive to others' critiques and advice, a DEO engages her stakeholders and empowers her coworkers. She motivates greater commitment from all levels, encourages less bureaucracy, and stimulates improved performance. By elevating purpose above ego, she imparts greater meaning to everyone's work.[1]

Humility

Arrogance

Accept possibility of being wrong	Insist they are always right
Courteous and respectful	Disdainful of others
Tolerant	Self-righteous
Quiet confidence	Loud bravado
Gratitude	Entitlement

When a DEO admits to needing a coach or trainer, as Carl Bass and Jesse Ziff Cool do in their profiles, it doesn't demean or weaken them. Instead, it showcases their confidence and agility. It models for others how, why, and when to seek guidance and reinforces the value of seeing yourself as a work in progress.[2]

Higher purpose

A DEO doesn't build her company around herself. She builds it around an idea that's larger than anything she could accomplish on her own. When she expands her team, it's not to elevate her or expand her power; instead, it's because she's found team members who share her dream. They become collaborators, embracing the DEO's vision and working to attain the same ideal.

The combination of a common goal, engaged stakeholders, and a leader willing to share power and credit creates a more adaptable

and sustainable organization. Because leadership and participation is distributed to all levels, yet connected to a unifying vision, the company can adjust to challenges and volatility.

If the DEO leaves (which is less likely due to her greater attachment to the company), another will take her place with a minimum of disruption or surprises. Chances are that the new DEO will know the value of humility and will already be co-creating with her eventual replacement.

1 Alimo-Metcalfe, Beverly and John Alban-Metcalfe. *Engaging Leadership: Creating Organisations That Maximise the Potential of Their People.* CIPD. http://www.cipd.co.uk/NR/rdonlyres/F72D3236-E832-4663-ABEC-BCC7890DC431/0/Engaging_leadership_STF.pdf
2 Ou, Yi. "CEO Humility and Its Relationship with Middle Manager Behaviors and Performance: Examining the CEO-Middle Manager Interface" (PhD diss., Arizona State University, 2011) http://repository.asu.edu/attachments/56727/content/Ou_asu_0010E_10748.pdf

Workouts to improve your humility

Stop talking.

The next time you find yourself in a battle of egos, try this: stop talking and let the other person dominate. By intentionally giving up the spotlight, your stress level will drop and your sense of control will rise.

Hold back.

Similarly, try not speaking first or last in any discussion. Each of these positions has an unfair advantage. The first to speak can sway others. The last to speak can take a position that benefits from hearing what everyone else has said. By choosing the middle you're risking having less impact and being an outlier—a position that's quite comfortable for someone practicing humility.

Care more.

Interview your colleagues as though you were writing their autobiographies. Ask questions about their childhood, their early influences, why they took one path versus another, what their talents are and how they developed them. Listen for the story rather than the answers. This simple tactic of seeing people's humanity can rightsize your ego and improve your relationships.

Give back.

Take responsibility for serving others in some part of your life. At work, this could mean bringing in new information, recommending local attractions, or running the sports betting pools. In your personal life, it could be volunteering in a soup kitchen, joining a group that cleans up beaches, or teaching English to immigrants. Whatever you do, regard your role as a servant to a greater good.

GO DEEPER

Being Wrong: Adventures in the Margin of Error by Kathryn Schulz
Humilitas: A Lost Key to Life, Love, and Leadership by John Dickson
The Servant: A Simple Story about the True Essence of Leadership by James C. Hunter
Good to Great: Why Some Companies Make the Leap ... and Others Don't by Jim Collins

Emily Pilloton

Executive Director of Project H Design
Director of Creativity at REALM Charter School

On one arm Emily Pilloton wears colorful string bracelets woven by her students. On the other she wears a sleekly designed Nike GPS watch. Like all DEOs, she is a study in contrasts. A self-admitted nerd who loves math and art. A teacher who loves structure and chaos. A woman who is empathetic and fierce.

We met Pilloton on a warm evening in an Oakland neighborhood café. Although tired from weeks of running her newest venture, Studio G, she took time to share the story of her young but impressive career.

Can you recall any early childhood experiences that shaped you?

I grew up in a house in the woods and spent most of my days building tree houses, naming rocks, and building forts. My two younger sisters were my first creative collaborators in a way. Because our house was in the middle of nowhere, we had to make our own fun. I have beautiful memories of growing up in that house and being able to play and learn in really organic, unintentional ways. I imagine a lot of my design sensibilities and my love of architecture and place came from that.

I also grew up in the age of MacGyver and seeing his problem solving. I had a huge crush on him. I mean, I think you could argue that he was the original design thinker.

When did you first believe you could lead?

My sense of leadership really came more through others' validation rather than my own awareness. In elementary and middle school, I was a black sheep in a lot of ways. I was a big nerd and the only nonwhite kid in the class for a long time. I felt out of place except when I played tennis. In my junior year of high school, my team had to select a captain. I didn't really think that was something I wanted to do, but then everyone silently voted for me to be the team captain. So I was like, oh, well, maybe people don't think I'm such a weirdo. Others saw potential in me that I hadn't seen in myself.

Why did you start your first company?

I had close to $100,000 in loans to pay off after graduate school. I went the traditional path and got a job designing furniture and working for an architecture firm just to pay my bills. That didn't last very long. I realized quickly that I don't do well working for other people. I have some problems with authority. I really just want to do my own thing.

I was disenchanted with the idea of working for seven different bosses, and with doing projects that didn't have my own heart and soul in them—like choosing doorknobs and other such ridiculous things. It didn't feel very important and it felt disconnected from who I was, the things I believed in, and the power I knew design could have in the world.

So I left the real world of having a job and a 401(k) and started a nonprofit. I didn't know any other way than to just try to figure it out, so I wrote the articles of incorporation for a nonprofit called Project H. The mission statement originally was rooted in four H words: humanity, habitat, health, and happiness. I had this inkling that there were other young designers who probably felt the same way.

"

It's important to fail because you'll learn from it, but in my mind, that's not really a failure.

"

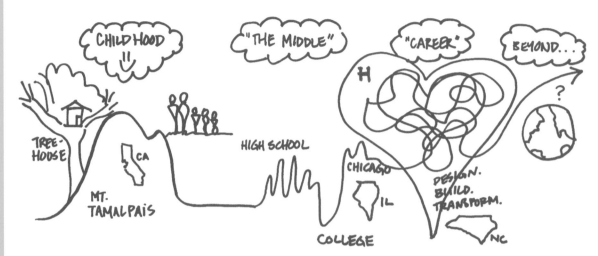

Emily travels from her tree house to a career in transformations.

Did you face any barriers in starting Project H?

Sure, like suddenly you have to raise money. I spent the first six months sending cold-call emails to people I admired or people I wanted to work with—people like Cameron Sinclair and Architecture for Humanity. He let me work in their space and people would come in and out of there, and I would talk to them. When anyone I came across seemed even remotely interested, I would email them. Maybe 30 percent of them responded.

The only way I knew to start was just to start having conversations, and then things started to stick. It was one of those things where I felt like if I led with confidence (even if I was faking it), at least I'd be in the right scenarios to figure it out. I discovered within the first month that I wasn't alone. There were people I'd gone to grad school with or people here in the Bay Area at CCA (California College of the Arts) or the Academy of Art

or UC Berkeley who were feeling the same kind of disenchantment with the design industry as we know it. Finding this sense of community helped. Even though I didn't know what projects might come of it, I knew there were others like me.

I still don't know what I'm doing all the time right now, but I have that first year to thank for building a sense of community and projects that turned into even bigger projects that have sustained us for a long time.

When did you start teaching creativity?

At the very beginning, we started working with groups around the world on a really local level, just trying to inject a creative process to produce solutions that were meaningful to people. I wrote the book *Design Revolution* and toured the country in an Airstream trailer that we turned into an exhibition space.

We let people engage and play with the designs, and we added some lectures and workshops around the power of design. We went everywhere, from the best design schools to random elementary schools in the middle of Louisiana. It was a great way to learn what this kind of work means in the bigger sphere, beyond the design community and my own little organization.

In the spring of 2009, I got this random email from a superintendent named Dr. Chip Zullinger, who was the superintendent of a school district in northeastern North Carolina called Bertie County. The whole northeastern part of the state is really rural and really poor, and this district in particular was struggling. Dr. Z reached out to us after seeing the Learning Landscape, an educational playground we designed that could be built in a day for free.

Over the course of two weeks, my partner and I got the email, booked flights, and flew to this place that's in the middle of nowhere. We built four playgrounds in four days. We then did six or seven more projects with him. After nine or ten months of traveling back and forth we pitched the idea of us becoming high school teachers. We figured that if we really wanted to be serious about design in public education, we needed to be in the classroom.

Were you confident this would work?

We were totally naive about what that involved. We pitched the idea that we'd bring back vocational education, but with a twist. We'd teach the hard skills—construction, masonry, carpentry, welding, digital fabrication, graphic design—all these things that were really relevant within industries, but then we'd infuse them with two things new to vocational education: design and a focus on community. We'd ask our students to design something the community needed and then build it.

But while creativity is natural to me, it became very clear that it was not natural to the students. I'd have these fifteen-, sixteen-, seventeen-year-olds who had gone through years of education that drained the creativity out of them. We may as well have been teaching them Arabic or something. It's so completely outside of their mode of operation. They looked at me like I was crazy, but the minute they started to see their ideas come to life at full-scale, that was the moment where I think they realized this isn't just about models on a desk. As a group, I think that was the biggest moment for them.

What would you say was your biggest mistake and what did you learn from it?

The whole discourse around failure and mistakes I think is almost a misnomer. It's important to fail because you'll learn from it, but in my mind, that's not really a failure. All you're doing is acting and making a decision and responding to it. Sometimes a decision has negative consequences. Sometimes there are positive consequences. But I almost don't even view them as mistakes or failures. They are things that happened that I had to respond to.

There are certainly projects that we've done that haven't turned out well. When we first got started as a nonprofit, we worked with this group in South Africa on a water transport device called the Hippo Roller. We partnered with an organization to redesign it. But we didn't have a lot of foresight about how tough it would be to manage a project that was so product centric and a world away, where you're not really connected to the place. That project was a failure, but in the best way because it helped us find our way and take on other projects.

Has your leadership style evolved?

I don't often think of my leadership skills or lack of skills in a focused way, but teaching has influenced how I lead. I'm definitely a control freak in some ways, but having to stand in front of a class of young people every day and be both compassionate and a disciplinarian moderates that. I think I've gotten a lot better at dancing the line between the hug and the smack upside the head, and that's a constant balance. I think kindness always rules, but every now and then you have to put your foot down. Being a woman, my nature is to be compassionate, but there are times when I'm like, okay, get your shit together.

My latest venture, Studio G, is the first time I've had to curate a team, not just work with one other partner. I needed to hire seven people who were all different, amazing, and worked well together. I had to give up a lot of what I wanted, but I got things from my team that I couldn't get otherwise.

How do you lead in a time of so much change?

The whole idea of leadership is kind of secondary to me—it's never really been my goal. The part of design that I really like is the intimacy of it. I like being in spaces where the design process can be really intimate, where you know the details of your student's family, and you can work with them on something that they want to create.

Education is a really tumultuous space, and it can feel really overwhelming, but when you're sitting next to a twelve-year-old who wants to build a floating island in the middle of the ocean, there's something really sweet and simple about it too. I try to seek out those opportunities that feel really intimate, but that are part of something that's a lot bigger.

Maybe that's what makes me a good leader—having those one-on-one experiences. I don't ever want to be in a position where I don't have that.

What do you love about your current job?

I love the intense intimacy of the work. When I was working in North Carolina, I would go home crying and come to school the next day totally rejuvenated. Now the context is different, but the feeling and the heart of it is very similar. It's obviously a more complex urban environment. There's just more of everything: more kids, more social workers, more drugs, more baggage that kids come to school with. But it all boils down to those small moments and that's what I try to focus on.

What's your superpower or key strength and what's your Kryptonite?

My Kryptonite for sure is that I'm impatient. If I start something, I'm damn well going to finish it. If my progress is held up, it drives me berserk. I'm also learning to delegate. Just yesterday I was thinking, "Why should I walk someone through my accounting system when I could do it myself in two hours while drinking coffee?" Then I realize that I need to grow up and have a real bookkeeping system.

As for my strength, I think I'm pretty good at keeping people motivated across a range of abilities. In my current program we have everything from high-performing students to ones who come twice a week if we're lucky. I can inspire both ends of that spectrum. I'm a good listener with students and other people.

Teaching a young girl how to handle power tools.

Do you have a company culture?

My motto was always "designing with people instead of for people." Now I'd say it's "designing *with* and *for* and *by* people." It's not just about me and my design, but about how can I support others so they can design for themselves.

Also, I emphasize systems, not stuff. There's design porn everywhere—sleek, shiny things. To me that just feels like you're missing the whole story of where the design came from and the people who are going to use it. I'm more interested in design that's sometimes invisible, that isn't a product, but rather this wonderful process that someone's really thought through that makes people's lives easier and more beautiful or more loving. I think design is so synonymous with the "thing," like the iPod, that it's hard to separate the two.

Do you think innovation depends more on process or people?

Our process is that there is no process. We defer to our students because we want them to have their own processes. But our approach is still rigorous. No matter what we're doing, you're going do it a hundred times. You're going to be better for it, for having done it ninety-nine more times than you wanted to. That's a tough sell to a seventeen-year-old, but I really love it when you're getting somewhere just by doing the work.

I've never really had a plan for our company. People will ask me what my five-year plan is and I tell them to ask me in four years. That sounds horrible, but I think especially in my own career, I want the flexibility to discover what's out there and be able to do that and not have a board of trustees that stops me because it's not in my strategic plan. Everything we've done that's special or successful or extraordinary has been a happy accident. Our design process embraces spontaneity and I want to be able to do that with my organization.

What three things do you want to be known for?

If someone describes me as all heart, I'll feel like that was the best thing ever. Also that I was fearless and that I was flawed. I mean I think that's kind of an asset as a leader—acknowledging that it's all a work in progress. The design work, the life work, isn't that what design is—just trying to make everything better every step of the way? I think that's true for my life, too. I keep making mistakes and then trying to correct them, and then I'll make another one. I think that's what makes it really fun.

GENEROSITY

Generosity is often equated with charity. It evokes the image of Daddy Warbucks magnanimously sharing his wealth with the destitute Little Orphan Annie. DEOs are generous, but they don't see themselves as modern-day benefactors of the less fortunate. DEOs give because it's creative.

We're trained as children to share, to be generous, and to let others use our toys. This requires repeated instruction, because sharing something means we get less of it for ourselves. It diminishes our control and ownership. This early training, while civilized and admirable, reinforces a worldview where resources are limited. The supply of money, time, and things is finite—a pie that cannot grow larger as it's divided into pieces.

This worldview persists as we grow older and are prompted to volunteer our time, pledge our money, and donate our unused stuff as a sign of our unselfishness or gratitude. In return, our generosity is acknowledged with plaques, goodie bags, and tax deductions. We may even gain an increased sense of well-being.[1]

Despite the early training, modest rewards, and psychic benefit, for most of us generosity remains a "should do" rather than a "must do." Giving is painful or inconvenient or unsatisfying. It's not nearly as buff and agile as its opposite—taking—an action that doesn't ask us to delay gratification or wait for the afterlife.

DEOs are no more virtuous or bighearted than the general population. They simply don't see giving as a zero-sum game with a winner and a loser. For a DEO, generosity is an investment with no downside. For a DEO, generosity creates more value than it gives away.

As Chris Anderson, the curator of TED, explains: "Just realize that we're in a time when an element of letting go can be unbelievably powerful. You let go in order to get back."

Infinite scale

A DEO's worldview recognizes that some resources are infinite. He has assets he can give away without losing possession of them. For example, unlike money, time, or tangible goods, information is infinitely extendable. Sharing it doesn't decrease his store of it. In fact, a DEO would argue that sharing information prompts diverse opinions and improves the overall level of discourse in a field.

Sharing connections by introducing friends and colleagues is another example of win-win generosity. Those introduced benefit from the new connection. The DEO reinforces his value to a network and encourages its growth and usefulness. As with information, a DEO does not lose a contact he shares.

Similarly, the concept of open source reflects the idea that a generously created resource can be shared infinitely to everyone's benefit. This approach runs rampant in the software and hardware industries, but it's also becoming more common in fields as disparate as beer, medicine, and fashion. Citizen science, citizen journalism, and open governance all rely on generous contributors building and sharing infinitely scalable resources.

"

That's what I consider true generosity: You give your all, and yet you always feel as if it costs you nothing.
Simone de Beauvoir

"

Reciprocity

Altruism is giving with no expectation of return—a saintly virtue hard to fault and equally hard to find. Most giving has some expectation of return, even if the return is just recognition. A DEO may or may not be altruistic depending on his personal ideals. But he wouldn't think of ignoring the value of reciprocal giving.

Unlike altruism, reciprocity is giving in order to get. Collaboration is a good example of reciprocity. A good collaborator provides help to others. He also expects to get help from others when he needs it. This is not predatory or manipulative. It's healthy. In companies where collaboration is standard, its benefits multiply exponentially, increasing profitability, productivity, and customer satisfaction.[2]

IDEO, one of the world's leading design firms, promotes a cultural value called "Make Others Successful." The firm's leader, Tim Brown,

A Hot Studio PhilathroParty would create competitions to see who could raise the most donations. Alcohol helped get everyone in a gift-giving mood.

recently explained that people obsessed with their own ideas aren't very good at collaborating with others. He goes on to explain how this attitude can win someone a job with his firm: "If they're generous with giving credit and talk about how someone else was instrumental in their progress, I know that they give help as well as receive it."

"Paying it forward" is another example of reciprocal generosity, although in this case, one person's generosity is passed along to someone else. Experienced executives mentoring startups for no return are paying forward the help they received earlier in their careers. An older female entrepreneur helping a younger one review a deal is paying forward an early break she received.

Generosity of this sort benefits from being structured and focused. Adam Grant, author of "In the Company of Givers and Takers" and an accomplished giver, explains that the most successful givers are strategic in their giving: they give to others who will reciprocate. They give to reinforce their connections and they give in ways that please them.[3] We would say they give like DEOs.

1 Aknin, Lara B., Christopher P. Barrington-Leigh, Elizabeth W. Dunn, John F. Helliwell, Justine Burns, Robert Biswas-Diener, Imelda Kemeza, Paul Nyende, Claire E. Ashton-James, and Michael I. Norton. "Prosocial Spending and Well-Being: Cross-Cultural Evidence for a Psychological Universal." *Journal of Personality and Social Psychology*, 104 (4), 635–52. doi: 10.1037/a0031578
2 Grant, Adam. April 2013. "In the Company of Givers and Takers." *Harvard Business Review.*
3 Grant, Adam M. Ph.D. 2013. *Give and Take: A Revolutionary Approach to Success.* New York: Viking Press.

Workouts to improve your generosity

Mentor someone.

Offer to share your knowledge and your contacts with no expectation of return. Make their success your sole goal. Appreciate acknowledgment if you get it, but don't expect it.

Find your voice.

Create a blog and set a goal to share some piece of information every day for a month. It's free on most platforms, easy to start, and you can always delete it later. If you're not good with words, choose a platform that lets you communicate through images or photos. Don't obsess over comments or shares. Your objective is to be generous with your expertise or knowledge, not to gain new fans.

Set it free.

Clean your garage or closet and list everything you're not using on Craigslist under the Free heading. If you live in a large city, just leave it on the street with a sign "Help Yourself." This mundane, practical activity has several benefits. It creates more space, helps those in need and encourages generosity in others. Maybe it gets you into Heaven, but we can't guarantee that.

Share the wealth.

Hoarding connections that you don't have the time or inclination to support is miserly. The world does not have a shortage of people. Next time you're too busy to follow up on a connection, rather than putting it off until sometime in the future, pass it on to someone else.

GO DEEPER

Give and Take: A Revolutionary Approach to Success by Adam Grant
The Generosity Factor by Ken Blanchard and S. Truett Cathy
More or Less: Choosing a Lifestyle of Excessive Generosity by Jeff Shinabarger

ORIGINALITY

Original. This coveted description brands jeans, art, recipes, and even sin. It signifies something unique and not derivative, something rare or noteworthy. Originality is what others are drawn to copy or driven to acquire. But for a DEO, originality isn't a quest or a creative goal. For a DEO, being an original is the only option.

Most people pay lip service to being original. They post Apple's "Think Different" prose on the wall and praise uniqueness as necessary, but they shy away from it in practice. Although we're all born originals (at least until cloning becomes practical), we quickly discover the high cost of maintaining our individuality. Social, educational, and business processes are set up to encourage and reward status quo thinking and behavior. Fitting in requires much less effort than standing out.

Being original is also risky. Ironically, this seems even more true in businesses going through transition or struggling to remain competitive. Andrew S. Allen, founder and editor of the movie review site *Short of the Week,* compared the originality of top-grossing movies from 1981 to 2011. In 1981, seven of the 10 highest-grossing movies were original stories. In 2011, none were. The rewards of conformity—in this case, releasing a sequel or a remake—are far more predictable and assured.

But none of this matters to a DEO. If she ever considered being normal or average, it was a brief flirtation.

To a DEO, originality doesn't mean adopting a counterculture or eccentric stance. It doesn't mean rebelling against everything or morphing into whichever persona is currently popular. Her originality comes from successfully integrating her full range of interests, talents, and traits, including those that seem contradictory. It comes from embracing her passions and preferences regardless of how the rest of the world reacts.

For Carl Bass and Ayah Bdeir, originality comes from integrating their love of analytics and art, two disciplines that usually require separate college campuses. For Chris Anderson and Jesse Ziff Cool, it comes from being both introverted and extroverted, a combination that doesn't even exist by most people's standards. For this book's authors, it comes from combining what are traditionally viewed as feminine and masculine leadership traits. By refusing to conform to narrow stereotypes and insisting on the legitimacy of their oddly aligned characteristics, DEOs create complex, unique personalities that are easy to admire and difficult to copy.

While being original is unavoidable to a DEO, it remains daunting. Originality requires courage and vulnerability: courage to express that which is unusual or unheeded and vulnerability to others' dismissal or ridicule. Particularly early in her career, a DEO must face these challenges largely alone. Few, if any, mentors or role models exist to lead the way. No guidelines or behavioral boundaries define the difference between admirably original and unconvincingly fragmented.

Fortunately, benefits and fans accrue over time. Being distinct and original helps a DEO stand out from the competition. It makes her more noteworthy and gets her more press. It attracts supporters who don't ask her to change and stakeholders who don't want her to leave. On a personal level, embracing and maintaining originality helps a DEO develop a sense of security and self-confidence that's based on a permanent quality. She's not afraid of losing her edge—of not being creative enough—because it is her essence, not just her skill set.

> "
> # Originality is independence, not rebellion; it is sincerity, not antagonism.
> George Henry Lewes
> "

Being original is associated with the ability to make independent judgments and not be swayed by others' opinions. Those who are comfortable with their originality tend to also be comfortable with self-assertion and as a result are better able to lead others.[2] This doesn't mean they are immune to criticism or failure. As Steve Gundrum, inventor extraordinaire at Mattson, confesses: "My ideas get shot down all the time and always have. … Luckily, I've never been blocked from expressing my creative vision."

Of course, it's impossible to be original in every characteristic and every endeavor. In fact, it's more likely that every idea builds from others' earlier efforts and inspiration. DEOs don't force originality for its own sake. It emerges naturally. In addition to a genetic disposition and a lucky upbringing, originality demands mastery, adaptability, and curiosity. A DEO may not start life with all these attributes, but she gains them over time and practices them daily.

Mastery

Being original usually takes a good deal of work. While a DEO may be born with an aptitude for combining math and fashion, these tendencies remain nothing more than inclinations unless she pursues a career that builds and integrates them.

Mastery comes from years of study and practice. It comes from a deep understanding of where concepts originate, why current behaviors exist, and what came before. This knowledgeable perspective is essential to the creation of original content. Understanding the roots of an industry enables a DEO to know what is new, what is derivative, and what is an outright copy. Mastering her discipline not only helps her effectively combine disparate skills, but also find novel ways of applying them.

Adaptability

For most DEOs, originality emerges from adaptation. Born with a passion others don't yet share or an odd collection of skills and proclivities others don't yet value, a DEO adapts her abilities to suit her surroundings. She won't change who she is, but she'll apply herself in a way that others can better appreciate.

Emily Pilloton, founder of Project H, expressed her originality differently depending on where she was and what was needed. She adapted her offerings one way to a poor, rural community and another to a wealthy suburb. Mark Dwight continued adapting and adjusting his originality until he found his true calling running Rickshaw.

In many cases, it is a DEO's adaptability that keeps her and her company up to date. Originality is highly attractive to others as a template for their own work. Over time, every original person, product, or service is sure to be copied. The copies are usually poor, but sufficient to downgrade the original's uniqueness. To counter this, a DEO treats originality as a moving target, developing and renewing the qualities that most contribute to its distinctiveness.

Curiosity

Originality thrives on a steady stream of fresh learning, new connections, and novel insights, often prompted by a DEO's curiosity. Her curiosity feeds creativity and fuels problem solving. It uncovers opportunities and drives them forward. It's what prompts her to question, to doubt, and to investigate.

A DEO may start a conversation with an innocently posed *what's that?* Before long, if the topic is anywhere close to something she's studying, the dialogue will quickly become intense and detailed. She'll want to understand how it works, where it came from, and why it's different. She'll want to compare notes, exchange contacts, and start a conference.

1 Allen, Andrew S. January 2012. "Has Hollywood Lost Its Way?" Short of the Week. http://www.shortoftheweek.com/2012/01/05/has-hollywood-lost-its-way/
2 Csikszentmihalyi, Mihaly. 1996. *Creativity: Flow and the Psychology of Discovery and Invention.* New York: HarperCollinsPublishers.

Workouts to improve your originality

Mash it up.

Make a list of what you love doing and what you hate doing. Cross out the list of what you hate doing and group the things you love doing according to their similarities. Label each group with a term that describes its contents. Now combine two groups that are dissimilar. This should produce a fairly original combination of activities you love. Do them more often.

Mind the gap.

All of us have something we'd love to do but have never learned. Fill that gap, no matter how unrelated it is to what you currently do. In fact, the more unrelated it is, the better.

Give up control.

If you have young children, spend time letting them be in charge—not running the household, but letting them decide what games to play, what rules to follow, and how to win. They're creative geniuses and can teach originality far better than adults.

Stand out.

Become known for something highly individual at work. Matthew Carlson, formerly at Hot Studio and now at Facebook, became one of the most prolific "pinners" on Pinterest (and one of the few men). By pursuing his interest despite its unusual nature, he gained notoriety not only within his company, but also in a much larger networked community.

GO DEEPER

Creativity: Flow and the Psychology of Discovery and Invention by Mihaly Csikszentmihalyi
Curious?: Discover the Missing Ingredient to a Fulfilling Life by Todd B. Kashdan
Pathfinders: A Global History of Exploration by Felipe Fernández-Armesto
The Dynamics of Creation by Anthony Storr
Creating Minds by Howard E. Gardner

When the SXSW crowds leave Austin in late March, the city returns to normal. The bars get quieter and the bands less numerous. Hotel rooms become affordable and restaurants lose their lines. The masses who came seeking change return home to share what they found and continue their search.

In a small office on Brazos Street, a few blocks from the Colorado River, a young DEO returns to his startup. Noah Zandan began his career on a more predictable path. He trained as an economist, interned with Lehman Brothers, and spent two years with Deutsche Bank Securities. He could have weathered the crash and grown wealthy on its upside, continuing to watch numbers flow across computer screens and advising others when to buy and sell. But Zandan has a creative side, and it wasn't happy on Wall Street.

Rather than use his quantitative mindset for personal gain, Zandan imagines a world where anyone can access, understand, and honestly reflect on information and data that is readily available to them. He believes that the combination of evidence and innovation will produce a happier, healthier, and more efficient and effective society. He wants to be part of the community that's enabling this future, so, spurred by advice from other startups, he merged his analytical skills and creative impulses to found Quantified Impressions, a company whose first product helps people communicate more accurately and authentically by analyzing their speaking voices.

On a distant stage, surrounded by politicians and journalists, another young DEO courageously raises her voice and continues risking her life. Sixteen-year-old Malala Yousafzai could have lived quietly and conservatively in her native Pakistan, performing traditional domestic chores. But Yousafzai has a warrior side, and it wasn't happy in the kitchen. She wants young girls to attend school without the fear of being killed. She wants children everywhere to have free access to education. She welcomes and incites this change with her simple plea, "Let us pick up our books and our pens. They are our most powerful weapons. One teacher, one book, one pen can change the world."

Yousafzai commands respect and holds attention not because she's precocious or gifted, but because her positive passion reaches out to millions of people and unites them in a shared goal. Her "startup" is her vision of safe, accessible education for children around the world. Her sales force will be the global community she coalesces. She will lead and inspire teams who learn from one another and who collaborate easily and effectively. She will be their role model of resilience, helping all who follow her to withstand failure and to evolve with the changes taking place around them.

In a once-dangerous section of downtown San Francisco, a team works to build a college that Yousafzai and Zandan would want to attend. Its founder, Ben Nelson, believes that he can combine the harmony of in-person social interaction with the lyrics of online learning. He believes that technology can help professors customize and extend their impact while it helps students better appreciate their strengths and accommodate their weaknesses. He believes that the ideal college experience mixes dorm life with virtual communities and scatters both across multiple countries.

The team that's building the Minerva Schools at KGI with Nelson isn't obsessed with growth projections, profit analyses, or IPO offerings. They're not testing taglines and landing pages. They're focused on creating an Ivy League-style university that will attract the world's best professors and most talented students. If they succeed, Minerva will be graduating DEOs by 2019.

Zandan, Yousafzai, and the Minerva entrepreneurs are devoting their energies to different problems at different scales, but they share the same mindset and a similar motivation. Like all DEOs, they're creating a concept of the future, iterating with products or services that move us forward. They share a quiet dissatisfaction with the status quo and a realistic recognition of the many ailments plaguing the world. Their unique form of protest is to fix the problems.

"
Always do whatever's next.
George Carlin
"

These are our new leaders, the people whose vision and vocabularies will shape our future. They are striving to find a balance between business as usual—which they know doesn't work—and the chaos of change and creativity. They hope to find that balance in their work and in their personal lives. Eventually they hope to find it in the world they co-create with everyone else.

DEOs are not infallible. They are not gods or superheroes with powers to fix every problem. A DEO will have as many flaws as a CEO; their flaws will just be different ones, ones less likely to cause global catastrophes in our interconnected world. Because DEOs are capable of distributing power and are sensitive to interdependencies, they're unlikely to build centralized systems with domino-like alignments that collapse with scant warning. Because DEOs accept the value of data *and* dreams, they're less likely to push an excess of environment-damaging freedoms or soul-sagging controls.

The problems they will address could fill volumes. They need to find the balance between privacy and transparency, between surveillance and security. They need to continue pulling people out of poverty without putting them into a lifestyle that consumes the planet's limited sources of water and food. They need to reverse climate change, eradicate inequality, and end war.

These challenges would intimidate any generation of leaders and perhaps, ultimately, this generation's leaders will fail too. But they will try, and in trying they will learn and share. With networks that stretch beyond any previous boundaries—beyond walls, cities, even continents—their learning can spread quickly and others can build on their experiments. Networked together, far-flung DEOs can collaborate on an improved version of the future, set in an unpredictable, fast-moving, and value-charged world that feels perfectly normal to them.

As we bring this book to a close, we'd like to begin a conversation. The qualities and characteristics we've outlined are only a prompt. Perhaps we've missed something. Perhaps we overemphasized one trait and underemphasized another. We know this topic is too big to be covered completely—in all its dimensions—in one book. We also know it's changing and evolving. We invite you to join in the discussion and hope you'll be part of this conversation and a participant in its evolution. www.riseofthedeo.com

Thank you,

*"The future belongs
to those who believe in the
beauty of their dreams."*

ELEANOR ROOSEVELT

Maria Giudice

Director of Product Design at Facebook

Christopher Ireland

Cofounder of Mix and Stir Studio

Maria and Christopher sit side by side in the playfully furnished lobby at Hot Studio. They've taught together for years and enjoy an easy, genuine friendship. Maria's pink-streaked hair frames a generous smile that matches her outgoing, expressive nature. Christopher's appearance is more reserved, but she's confident and relaxed in the bustling, fast-paced creative studio.

Both women have spent their careers learning to lead in the midst of constant change. They've built companies whose success depended upon attracting and keeping talented professionals. They learned to course correct quickly, collaborate widely, and fail effectively. They built cultures friendly to marriage and children. After a decade and a half of passionate, values-driven leadership, each successfully sold her company and began again on a new adventure.

As a child, did you know what you'd be when you grew up?

Maria: I was really fortunate as a child because I always knew what I wanted to be. As early as I can remember I wanted to be an artist—a famous artist. In my sixth-grade yearbook each student was asked, "What are you going to grow up to be?" My answer was "either a famous artist or Raquel Welch look-alike." Those were my two trajectories in life. The breasts never came, sadly, so I had to fall back on the career as an artist. I thought I was going to be a painter, but through college and other experiences in my life, I turned into a graphic designer.

Christopher: I had several things that I thought I'd be when I grew up. The most outlandish, for me, at the time was an astronaut. It's outlandish because I wasn't even tall enough to be a flight attendant. I also don't like to fly and I had no background in science. I just thought it would be fun. In quick succession after that, I wanted to be a mom, a teacher, and then my favorite career, a hairdresser.

Maria: Even though I knew very early on that I wanted to be an artist, what I hadn't yet realized was my entrepreneurial spirit. I only realized that much later on in life through reflection. I was an accidental entrepreneur. I've always had the ability to fend for myself. I had to be successful on my own, so I always had a mindset of sustainability and, as I got older, the entrepreneurial spirit and the design spirit kind of combined into the leader that I am today. I used creativity and my design sense to find my path. There was no guidebook on how to get here.

Christopher: This is one of the interesting things about our friendship. Maria and I are exact opposites in some ways. I didn't know what I wanted to be until I was 29 or 30. It took me that long to try out all the different options and figure out that being an astronaut was not for me. Eventually I realized that I wasn't going to be happy in life until I could be creative. Much of my searching was just looking for a job that would let me be who I was. As a woman, those options were really limited at the time.

I think part of why Maria and I align is that, as women, we were shaped by similar forces. We had to invent a lot of the things we pursued. Maria always had a creative drive, and discovered entrepreneurialism later. I always had an entrepreneurial drive, and discovered creativity later. We've had very different career trajectories, but we wound up valuing the same traits, supporting the same behaviors, and seeing the same future.

"

Creativity is being able to constantly accept what's coming at you.

"

Christopher navigates a career that
spirals through highs and lows,
loves and losses.

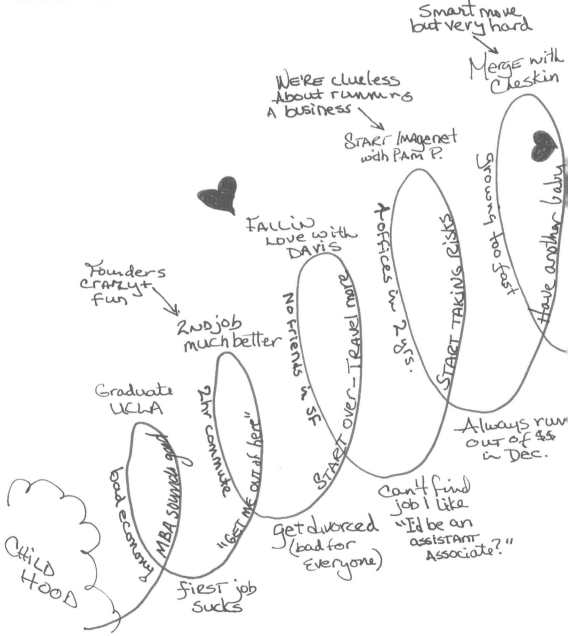

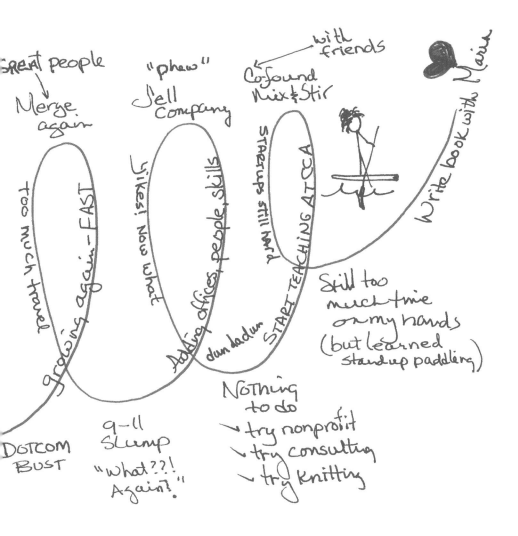

GREAT people

Merge again

"phew"

Jell Company

with friends

Cofound Mix & Stir

Maine

too much travel

growing again—FAST

Yikes! Now what

doing offices, people skills

dum da dum

STARTUPS still hard

START TEACHING AT CCA

Write book with

Still too much time on my hands (but learned standup paddling)

Nothing to do
↘ try nonprofit
↘ try consulting
↘ try knitting

DOTCOM BUST

9-11 Slump

"What??! Again?"

Christopher is A Girl.
This is her career drawing.

189

When did you first realize you could lead?

Maria: At the Understanding Business early in my career, I was in charge of designing maps, and as the department grew, I accidentally became a creative director for over twenty people in the course of one year. That experience helped me realize that I had a knack for organizing people, setting priorities, and motivating them in a way to produce their best work. The job came very naturally to me.

Christopher: I'm the oldest of seven children, all born within ten years. I could lead from my crib. I wasn't always a good leader. When I was young, I thought good leadership was figuring out how to make my siblings do things I was smart enough not to do. Hopefully, I've outgrown that.

Has your leadership style evolved?

Maria: I think being a parent changes you a lot as a leader. I think once you become a mother, you realize there's more to life than just a P&L. There are soft things that matter in life, like time and motivation—qualities you hope your children will develop will impact the kind of leader you are.

Christopher: I agree. I could never compartmentalize my lives. I couldn't be one person at home and one person at work. Sometimes my family had to adjust. I'm known for having a very, very organized house. That's my CEOness coming out in the house. On the other hand, in running my first company, Cheskin, I really cared about the people who worked there. It mattered to me that they were secure. It mattered to me that they were becoming better at their jobs and better people over time.

> "
> # When you're a leader, the higher up you are, the bigger mistakes you make.
> "

Maria: When I think of the people at Hot Studio, I realize that this was a group of people I only had for a moment in time. Eventually our employees will go somewhere else. And so for me, what I consider a great mark of leadership is what people do after they leave Hot Studio. Can we grow the next generation of creative leaders and can they do great things after this?

How do you recognize creativity in others?

Maria: I look for creativity in every person. My philosophy is that you're born with creativity, and then through the course of your life sometimes the creativity is beaten out of you. I really believe that there's creativity in any kind of job, whether it's accounting or HR or design. There's this creative spirit that enables people to not necessarily follow the rules, but to carve their own path based on what makes sense by looking at research, identifying patterns, figuring out what people really need, and having that sense of intuition to move something forward. Having a combination of curiosity and intuition, mapped with analytical skills, is a good balance of what

I would define as a really creative person. I also think creative people are really comfortable with uncertainty because they're constantly inventing and reinventing and breaking things down and trying new things. I look for that kind of energy and that way that people are thinking out loud.

Christopher: Quickness is one indication, to me. How quickly they grasp ideas. How diversely they think about those ideas. How they replay those ideas to others. How they mix ideas together. Resourcefulness is another trait. I love to watch people problem solve. I love to give them any kind of problem, even if it's an impossible one, and just see how they play with it. The most creative people, I think, tend to not get flustered when you ask them why. If they see a problem, they just dive in and keep trying different approaches until they figure it out.

What do you love about your job?

Maria: Well, since I've just started working at Facebook, that question is a little hard to answer. One thing that Hot Studio and Facebook have in common is the fact that I get to work with some of the most talented, creative people in the world every single day. Even though I've already had a long career, I get to learn and try to solve new problems. I get exposed to new things and people who will challenge my assumptions about the way I look at the world around me. Creative people feed my soul.

Christopher: I agree. I love the continual opportunity to learn. Every project, every meeting, every event—I almost always learn something. Every job becomes a living project for me where I'm tweaking and experimenting. If I learn something one day, the next day I'll be trying to apply it. When I ran Cheskin, I'd come into the office and say, "Can't we rearrange the desks this way?

Can't we set up our computer system this way? Can't we rethink how we do our marketing?" It would drive people crazy sometimes because they felt like there was never a time when we weren't changing. But I credit our success to that. I think, otherwise, you just fall behind really fast. Nowadays, you have to change constantly so you might as well get in the mode of learn, change, learn, change, learn, change.

How did you spur innovation in your companies?

Maria: Experiment and allow failure. I've done a lot of experiments that have gone terribly wrong. But I'm okay with it. People are like, "Uh, this is the worst thing we ever did. Let's not do that again." I'm like, "Yeah, I guess we won't do it again. That really sucked. But at least we tried it. And it's okay to do that." I think it's important to teach people that it's okay to try things that could be great failures, just not failures big enough to lose your business. It's a fine point, but it gives people permission to make mistakes. And when you're a leader, the higher up you are, the bigger mistakes you make.

Christopher: At Cheskin we lived by the saying "Evolve or die." We even included it in everyone's annual review. By that we meant that you simply have to keep up and continually improve. You can't sit in your corner and practice your craft by yourself. Creativity is being able to constantly accept what's coming at you: all the new technology, all the new tools, all the new cultures and foreign markets that are opening up. You have to figure out how to integrate that into what you do. You have to figure out how to still be creative and professional and productive with everything that's being thrown at you.

Maria charts her course early, takes risks often, and builds a career that suits her head and her heart.

CHILDHOOD Staten Island, NY

painting lessons every Sat. morn

first commission- dog portrait painting

80's Cooper Union NYC!

obsessions: Rocky Horror Prince

senior year met Richard Saul Wurman

inspired me!

get 1st job @ Access Press designing guidebooks

90's FREELANCE

work on Agfa guidebooks w/ Gene & Sanjay

become huge hits

form YO w/ Lynne Stiles

meet hot guy rollerblading

start a new company

hot DOT.COM BOOM

marries M! in 1999

hot

Hot grows to 75 people, well respected in industry

painted
jean jackets
in high
school

began
interest
in lettering

sign
painting

band
posters

calligraphy

RSW opens
TUB in SF—
accidentally
moves to SF
to work on
Yellow Pages

maps

Love the
MAC! Move
from analog
to digital

build kickass
cartography
dept. Embrace
collaborative
design &
leadership

WWW.
get into web
design early

coauthor
"Elements of
Web Design"

partnership
ends in
1997

Company
grows from
6 to 20 in a
few months!

have a baby
MAX
2000

dot com
BUST

Lots of ups & downs

have
Olivia
in 2003

acquisition!
to Facebook
In
2013

Now Director
of
Product
Design

future
looks bright!

How do you validate risks?

Maria: I've been in business for twenty years now, so I feel really good about my intuition. I think that longevity gives me a free pass when I'm making decisions. So I have that in my favor. But the way I validate is throwing a lot of ideas out and asking for feedback. I really believe in diverse opinions. I really believe in having a leadership team that is multidisciplinary, that has different points of view that challenge my ideas. They may not change my mind, but it gives me a perspective that I might not have had otherwise. I don't believe in design by committee, but I definitely believe in soliciting feedback and appreciating other people's points of view. How I operate is almost like Judge Judy: I've gotten all the information and now I'm going to rule.

Christopher: Well, the standing joke with my friends and colleagues is that if I believe there's a 51 percent chance that my idea is going to work, then to me it's not a risk. Anything less than that, then yeah, maybe it's a little risky, but 51 percent—come on, let's go. I also believe that my attitude can make things happen. Not in an "I'm all powerful" way, but if I'm with the right people and we're all aligned and we're going after the same goal, then we can make it happen. It's hard to quantify what happens when you're really committed to pushing something through.

Have you overcome any hurdles in your career?

Maria: I think that women leaders have different obstacles than male leaders. Both of us have successfully raised children and have become leaders of organizations. When I was pregnant with my first child, I felt like I was going to be left behind for a little while because my priority was my family, my child. My commitment was to being a mother. I was present. I brought the baby to work. I limited my travel for a couple of years, because I care enough about being a parent, in addition to being a good leader. I think, with my two kids, that was a bit of an obstacle. It set me back in comparison to my competition.

Christopher: For me, being on the West Coast was an obstacle. Most of my clients and business opportunities were on the East Coast. Not being thought of as a technical company was an obstacle. Having to reinvent how people thought of the business I was in was a big obstacle because at the time, design research didn't even exist. It was market research or it was ethnography and nobody knew what user research was. Finally, the biggest problem, by far, was just finding really talented, dedicated people who could do the job, who were reliable, who were creative. It's still a very, very tough hurdle for any entrepreneur. But everyone has hurdles. That's what shapes the business.

How would you describe each other?

Maria: Even before we became good friends, I looked up to Christopher as an incredible leader, a female leader of an organization that was largely made up of men. I used to think she was much more buttoned up and all business, but now I know she's a free spirit. She's creative. She goes places that I don't go when it comes to creativity. When we work together, she throws out crazy ideas that I never think will work, and they become wildly successful. Another thing that I've really come to appreciate about Christopher is that she gets ahead of the curve. She understands trends. She understands human behavior.

Christopher: Maria is this amazing combination of opposites. She's fierce and yet compassionate. She's creative but very practical. She's warm and generous, but also cool and focused. Usually leaders are stereotypic. There are different types, but you can predict their character traits and put them in a box. Maria can't go in a box. She's also very brave—more than I am, I think. She has high integrity and she'll fight anyone for her values. She doesn't easily back down, but not because she's closed off or only heeds her own counsel. She's very open. These combinations make her really quite unique as an individual and as a leader.

What kind of culture did you create?

Maria: I've always believed in the power of the collective: more brains produce better ideas and better ideas create better solutions. At Hot Studio I built a culture of openness, honesty, and transparency. It was a place where people could work in an environment of co-creation, collaboration, and teamwork to produce outstanding, thought-provoking work.

Christopher: Cheskin was an ongoing, collaborative experiment that reflected the values of the people working there. I look back and say it was a performance. We took the stage each day and did hours of really amazing improv with new clients, new environments, and new challenges. We never had the details fully worked out, but we had principles that guided us. Those principles still guide me.

When you're gone from the scene, what three things do you want to be known for?

Maria: I try to be mindful and appreciate every single day that I am alive. Many years ago, my daughter fell off a bunk bed and got a very bad concussion. She could easily have died. That traumatic event reminds me how precious our time on Earth is and how important it is not to waste a single moment of it. I want people to

> "
> I love the continual opportunity to learn. Every project, every meeting, every event—I almost always learn something.
> "

remember that I've tried to live my life to the fullest each and every day. Second, that I inspired a whole generation of people to love what they do and be the best they can be, as creative people and as human beings. Finally, that I was a good, kind wife to my husband, Scott, and a role model and kick-ass mother to my two amazing children, Olivia and Max.

Christopher: Well, I hope that people would describe me as someone they loved collaborating with; someone who helped them do their very best work. I hope my family—Davis, Jeff, Kelley and MacKenzie—will say I lived a good life, that I was fair and generous and loving. Finally, I hope I've made some positive impact on the future. I don't know what it will be, but I hope something I've done makes a difference.

RESOURCES

Change

Who Moved My Cheese? by Spencer Johnson

Switch: How to Change Things When Change is Hard by Chip Heath and Dan Heath

Change by Design: How Design Thinking Transforms Organizations and Inspires Innovation by Tim Brown

Leading Change by John P. Kotter

Mindset: The New Psychology of Success by Carol S. Dweck

Risk

Against the Gods: The Remarkable Story of Risk by Peter L. Bernstein

Taking Smart Risks: How Sharp Leaders Win When Stakes are High by Doug Sundheim

Little Bets: How Breakthrough Ideas Emerge from Small Discoveries by Peter Sims

Decisive: How to Make Better Choices in Life and Work by Chip Heath and Dan Heath

Systems Thinking

Thinking in Systems: A Primer by Donella H. Meadows

Business Dynamics: Systems Thinking and Modeling for a Complex World by John D. Sterman

The Fifth Discipline: The Art and Practice of the Learning Organization by Peter M. Senge

Emergence: The Connected Lives of Ants, Brains, Cities, and Software by Steven Johnson

Out of Control: The New Biology of Machines, Social Systems, and the Economic World by Kevin Kelly

Freakonomics: A Rogue Economist Explores the Hidden Side of Everything by Steven D. Levitt and Stephen J. Dubner

Intuition

Thinking, Fast and Slow by Daniel Kahneman

Blink: The Power of Thinking without Thinking by Malcolm Gladwell

Intuition: Its Powers and Perils by David G. Myers

Strategic Intuition: The Creative Spark in Human Achievement by William Duggan

Social Intelligence

PeopleSmart: Developing Your Interpersonal Intelligence by Melvin L. Silberman

Social Intelligence: The New Science of Human Relationships by Daniel Goleman

The Power of the Herd: A Nonpredatory Approach to Social Intelligence, Leadership, and Innovation by Linda Kohanov

The Social Animal: The Hidden Sources of Love, Character, and Achievement by David Brooks

GSD

The 7 Habits of Highly Effective People: Powerful Lessons in Personal Change by Stephen R. Covey

The One-Minute Manager by Kenneth Blanchard, Ph.D. and Spencer Johnson, M.D.

Getting Things Done: The Art of Stress-Free Productivity by David Allen

Co-Creation

Wikinomics: How Mass Collaboration Changes Everything by Donald Tapscott and Anthony D. Williams

The Wealth of Networks: How Social Production Transforms Markets and Freedom by Yochai Benkler

Group Genius: The Creative Power of Collaboration by Keith Sawyer

Crowdsourcing: Why the Power of the Crowd Is Driving the Future of Business by Jeff Howe

Networks & Communities

Connected: The Surprising Power of Our Social Networks and How They Shape Our Lives by Nicholas A. Christakis and James H. Fowler

Sync: How Order Emerges From Chaos In the Universe, Nature, and Daily Life by Steven H. Strogatz

Linked: How Everything Is Connected to Everything Else and What It Means for Business, Science, and Everyday Life by Albert-László Barabási

Mentoring

A Game Plan for Life: The Power of Mentoring by John Wooden and Don Yaeger

Monday Morning Leadership: 8 Mentoring Sessions You Can't Afford to Miss by David Cottrell

Mentoring: The Tao of Giving and Receiving Wisdom by Chungliang Al Huang and Jerry Lynch

Company Culture

Grow: How Ideals Power Growth and Profit at the World's Greatest Companies by Jim Stengel

Absolute Honesty: Building a Corporate Culture that Values Straight Talk and Rewards Integrity by Larry Johnson and Bob Phillips

The Designful Company: How to Build a Culture of Nonstop Innovation by Marty Neumeier

Care & Feeding of Employees

Love 'em or Lose 'em: Getting Good People to Stay by Beverly L. Kaye

Managing with Carrots: Using Recognition to Attract and Retain the Best People by Adrian Gostick and Chester Elton

The Carrot Principle: How the Best Managers Use Recognition to Engage Their People, Retain Talent, and Accelerate Performance by Adrian Gostick and Chester Elton

First, Break All the Rules: What the World's Greatest Managers Do Differently by Marcus Buckingham and Curt Coffman

Work Environment

Workplace by Design: Mapping the High-Performance Workscape by Franklin Becker and Fritz Steele

Best of Office Architecture and Design by Cindy Allen

Make Space: How to Set the Stage for Creative Collaboration by Scott Doorley and Scott Witthoft

I Wish I Worked There! A Look Inside the Most Creative Spaces in Business by Kursty Groves and Will Knight

Positive Passion

Lean In by Sheryl Sandberg

The Fred Factor: How Passion in Your Work and Life Can Turn the Ordinary into the Extraordinary by Mark Sanborn and John C. Maxwell

Work with Passion: How to Do What You Love for a Living by Nancy Anderson

Make the Impossible Possible: One Man's Crusade to Inspire Others to Dream Bigger and Achieve the Extraordinary by Bill Strickland and Vince Rause

Expertise

The Talent Code: Greatness Isn't Born. It's Grown. Here's How by Daniel Coyle

Practice Perfect: 42 Rules for Getting Better at Getting Better by Doug Lemov, Erica Woolway, and Katie Yezzi

Outliers: The Story of Success by Malcolm Gladwell

Problem Solving

Problem Solving 101: A Simple Book for Smart People by Ken Watanabe

The Thinker's Toolkit: 14 Powerful Techniques for Problem Solving by Morgan D. Jones

The Power of Thinking Differently: An Imaginative Guide to Creativity, Change, and the Discovery of New Ideas by Javy W. Galindo

Divergent Thinking (Creativity Research Series) by Mark A. Runco

Permission to Fail

Being Wrong: Adventures in the Margin of Error by Kathryn Schulz

Better by Mistake: The Unexpected Benefits of Being Wrong by Alina Tugend

The Power of Vulnerability: Teachings on Authenticity, Connection, and Courage by Brené Brown

Brilliant Mistakes: Finding Success on the Far Side of Failure by Paul J. H. Schoemaker

The Wisdom of Failure: How to Learn the Tough Leadership Lessons Without Paying the Price by Laurence G. Weinzimmer and Jim McConoughey

Playful Work

Play: How It Shapes the Brain, Opens the Imagination, and Invigorates the Soul by Stuart Brown

Homo Ludens: A Study of the Play-Element in Culture by Johan Huizinga

Creative Intelligence: Harnessing the Power to Create, Connect, and Inspire by Bruce Nussbaum

Iteration & Evolution

Organizations Evolving by Howard Aldrich and Martin Ruef

Dealing with Darwin: How Great Companies Innovate at Every Phase of Their Evolution by Geoffrey A. Moore

The Lean Startup: How Today's Entrepreneurs Use Continuous Innovation to Create Radically Successful Businesses by Eric Ries

The Science of Serendipity: How to Unlock the Promise of Innovation by Matt Kingdon

Integrity

Integrity: The Courage to Meet the Demands of Reality by Dr. Henry Cloud

The Integrity Dividend: Leading by the Power of Your Word by Tony Simons

Honest Business: A Superior Strategy for Starting and Managing Your Own Business by Michael Phillips and Salli Rasberry

True North: Discover Your Authentic Leadership by Bill George and Peter Sims

All Marketers Are Liars: The Underground Classic That Explains How Marketing Really Works—and Why Authenticity Is the Best Marketing of All by Seth Godin

Humility

Being Wrong: Adventures in the Margin of Error by Kathryn Schulz

Humilitas: A Lost Key to Life, Love, and Leadership by John Dickson

The Servant: A Simple Story about the True Essence of Leadership by James C. Hunter

Good to Great: Why Some Companies Make the Leap … and Others Don't by Jim Collins

Generosity

Give and Take: A Revolutionary Approach to Success by Adam Grant

The Generosity Factor: Discover the Joy of Giving Your Time, Talent, and Treasure by Ken Blanchard and S. Truett Cathy

More or Less: Choosing a Lifestyle of Excessive Generosity by Jeff Shinabarger

Originality

Creativity: Flow and the Psychology of Discovery and Invention by Mihaly Csikszentmihalyi

Curious? Discover the Missing Ingredient to a Fulfilling Life by Todd B. Kashdan

Pathfinders: A Global History of Exploration by Felipe Fernández-Armesto

The Dynamics of Creation by Anthony Storr

Creating Minds: An Anatomy of Creativity Seen Through the Lives of Freud, Einstein, Picasso, Stravinsky, Eliot, Graham, and Gandhi by Howard E. Gardner

References:

Adam M. Grant Ph.D. Give and Take: A Revolutionary Approach to Success

Aknin, Lara B., Christopher P. Barrington-Leigh, Elizabeth W. Dunn, John F. Helliwell, Justine Burns, Robert Biswas-Diener, Imelda Kemeza, Paul Nyende, Claire E. Ashton-James, and Michael I. Norton. "Prosocial Spending and Well-Being: Cross-Cultural Evidence for a Psychological Universal." *Journal of Personality and Social Psychology,* 104 (4), 635–52. doi: 10.1037/a0031578

Alimo-Metcalfe, Beverly and John Alban-Metcalfe. *Engaging Leadership: Creating Organisations That Maximise the Potential of Their People.* CIPD. http://www.cipd.co.uk/NR/rdonlyres/F72D3236-E832-4663-ABEC-BCC7890DC431/0/Engaging_leadership_STF.pdf

Allen, Andrew S. January 2012. "Has Hollywood Lost Its Way?" Short of the Week. http://www.shortoftheweek.com/2012/01/05/has-hollywood-lost-its-way/

Amabile, Teresa, and Steven Kramer. 2011. "Do Happier People Work Harder?" *New York Times,* September 3. http://www.nytimes.com/2011/09/04/opinion/sunday/do-happier-people-work-harder.html?_r=0

American Psychological Association. 2012. Psychologically Healthy Workplace Program. http://www.apaexcellence.org and Harvard Business School Press. 2004. *Coaching and Mentoring: How to Develop Top Talent and Achieve Stronger Performance.* Boston: Harvard Business School.

Atkinson, Martin. "The positive impact of office design." *FMLink.* http://www.fmlink.com/article.cgi?type=Magazine&title=The%20positive%20impact%20of%20office%20design&pub=Premises%20&%20Facilities%20Management&id=42382&mode=source

Atkinson, Philip E. 1990. *Creating Cultural Change: The Key to Successful Total Quality Management.* San Diego: Pfeiffer & Co.

Barsade, Sigal G. 2002. "The Ripple Effect: Emotional Contagion and Its Influence on Group Behavior." *Administrative Science Quarterly* 47 (4): 644–75.

Bialik, Carl. "Seven Careers in a Lifetime?" *Wall Street Journal,* September 4, 2010. http://online.wsj.com/article/SB10001424052748704206804576461628 05877990.html

Bransford, John D., ed. 2000. *How People Learn: Brain, Mind, Experience, and School,* expanded ed. Washington, DC: National Academy Press. http://www.napedu/openbook/0309070368/html/31html, copyright, 2000 The National Academy of Sciences

Brown, Stuart L. 2009. *Play: How It Shapes the Brain, Opens the Imagination, and Invigorates the Soul.* New York: Avery.

Covey, Stephen M. R. 2011. *The Speed of Trust: The One Thing That Changes Everything.* New York: Free Press.

Csikszentmihalyi, Mihaly. 1996. *Creativity: Flow and the Psychology of Discovery and Invention.* New York: HarperCollinsPublishers.

Fairlie, Robert W. 2012. *Kauffman Index of Entrepreneurial Activity, 1996–2011.* http://www.kauffman.org/uploadedFiles/KIEA_2012_report.pdf

Goleman, Daniel, Richard Boyatzis, and Annie McKee. 2002. *Primal Leadership: Realizing the Power of Emotional Intelligence.* Boston: Harvard Business School Press.

Grant, Adam. 2013. "Givers Take All: The Hidden Dimension of Corporate Culture." *McKinsey Quarterly.*

Grant, Adam. 2013. "Givers Take All: The Hidden Dimension of Corporate Culture." *McKinsey Quarterly,* April. http://www.mckinsey.com/insights/organization/givers_take_all_the_hidden_dimension_of_corporate_culture

Grant, Adam. April 2013. "In the Company of Givers and Takers." *Harvard Business Review.*

IBM Global Business Services. 2012. *Leading Through Connections: Insights from the IBM Global Chief Executive Officer Study.* http://www.ibm.com/ceostudy2012

Johnson, James E. May 30–31, 2007. "Play and Creativity." (Prepared for the Play and Creativity Conference, Tainan, R.O.C.)

Kolakowski, Nick. January 9, 2013. "The Billion-Dollar Startup: Inside Obama's Campaign Tech." Slashdot. http://slashdot.org/topic/bi/the-billion-dollar-startup-inside-obamas-campaign-tech/

Lehrer, Jonah. 2008. "The Eureka Hunt: Why Do Good Ideas Come to Us When They Do?" *The New Yorker,* July28. http://www.newyorker.com/reporting/2008/07/28/080728fa_fact_lehrer

Lloyd's. 2011. Lloyd's Risk Index. http://www.lloyds.com/news-and-insight/risk-insight/lloyds-risk-index

Lunenburg, Fred C. 2010. "Managing Change: The Role of the Change Agent." International Journal of Management, Business and Administration, Vol. 13, No. 1.

Marshall, Jessica. 2012. "Victory for Crowdsourced Biomolecule Design." *Nature,* January 22. doi:10.1038/nature.2012.9872.

Miron-Spektor, Ella, Miriam Erez, and Eitan Naveh. March 2012. "To Drive Creativity, Add Some Conformity." *Harvard Business Review.* http://hbr.org/2012/03/to-drive-creativity-add-some-conformity/ar/1

Murphy, Cliff. Reducing Risk and Increasing the Probability of Project Success. http://www.projectsmart.co.uk/reducing-risk-increasing-probability-of-project-success.html

O'Neill, Michael. 2010. Generational Preferences: A Glimpse into the Future Office. Knoll Workplace Research. http://www.kbmworkspace.com/pdf/A%20Glimpse%20into%20the%20Future%20Office.pdf

Ou, Yi. "CEO Humility and Its Relationship with Middle Manager Behaviors and Performance: Examining the CEO-Middle Manager Interface" (PhD diss., Arizona State University, 2011) http://repository.asu.edu/attachments/56727/content/Ou_asu_0010E_10748.pdf

PRWeek/Burson-Marsteller CEO Survey, 2007

Ries, Eric. 2011. *The Lean Startup: How Today's Entrepreneurs Use Continuous Innovation to Create Radically Successful Businesses.* New York: Crown Business.

Spencer, Stuart. *2004 CEO Study: A Statistical Snapshot of Leading CEOs.*

Surowiecki, James. 2004. *The Wisdom of Crowds.* New York: Doubleday.

The Authenticity Gap: Managing Expectations and Experience, 2012, FleishmanHillard

Vacharkulksemsuk, Tanya, Leslie E. Sekerka, and Barbara L. Fredrickson. 2011. "Establishing a Positive Emotional Climate to Create 21st-Century Organizational Change." In *The Handbook of Organizational Climate and Culture, 2nd ed.,* edited by Neal M. Ashkanasy, Celeste P M Wilderom, and Mark F. Peterson, 101–118. Thousand Oaks, California: Sage Publications.

Warrell, Margie. 2013. *Stop Playing Safe.* Milton, Australia: John Wiley & Sons.

WorkDesign magazine. July 2012. "The Benefits of Plants in the Workplace." http://workdesign.co/2012/07/the-benefits-of-plants-in-the-workplace/

INDEX

ACKNOWLEDGMENTS

We have a long list of people we wish to thank for their help and support in taking this book from a rough concept to a published book. Please join us in acknowledging the help and support of this fine cast of characters.

Christie Dames of TechTalk Studio suggested the initial idea to Maria and coined the phrase "DEO." Kevin O'Malley, also of TechTalk Studio, helped refine the idea and provided guidance and encouragement along the way. Janine Shiota provided early support for the idea of the DEO and had the courage to put Maria on the TedxPresidio conference stage in 2011, which propelled the development of this book.

To our profiled DEOs, we wish to extend separate thanks:

Carl Bass—thank you for sharing such personal and intimate insights with us.

Ayah Bdeir—we deeply appreciated your flexibility and gracious good nature.

Mark Dwight—thank you for letting us hang with you at Rickshaw and learn all your "Markisms."

Jesse Ziff Cool—thank you for the delicious lunch, yummy drinks and heartfelt sharing.

Steve Gundrum—we greatly appreciated your candid comments and shared memories of Wisconsin.

Emily Pilloton—thank you for sitting through two interviews in the midst of your very busy life.

Chris Anderson—much thanks and appreciation for years of fabulous TED conferences that inspired much of our thinking in this book.

We owe special thanks to Radhika Bhalia, our DEO researcher. Radhika not only helped source material for us, she participated in our brainstorms and interviewed us for our profile. Other significant Hot Studio contributors include Rajan Dev, who cheered us on and gave us the time and space to work on the book. Kelly Meanley and John Cantwell provided excellent marketing support. Another round of applause goes to all the Hot Studio employees who inspired Maria to create this book and who sat through constant iterations of her lectures that eventually formed the content.

Christopher's colleagues at Mix & Stir Studio were likewise patient and accommodating as she sat, earbuds in place, teasing out sentences that could bring this book to life.

This book would have languished without our girlfriend guidance network. Lisa Solomon, Lisa Gansky, and Nancy Duarte provided stellar advice on book publishing contracts and agents. Michelle Katz provided much needed review and advice on the antiquated legal language of publishing contracts. Honorary girlfriends Nathan Shedroff and Barry Katz also shared helpful publishing advice.

We greatly appreciate the partnership of Nancy Ruenzel and Michael Nolan from Peachpit Press. They fell in love with the idea of *Rise of the DEO* and took a tremendous risk by giving us complete control over the book's design, including the cover.

David Albertson guided the book's design. Special thanks to Paul Torres who put in numerous weekend hours to perfect the layout, color, and composition. Andrew Deming created the noteworthy information graphics throughout the book. Production designer wunderkind David Van Ness put the final touches on layout to get the book ready for press.

On a more personal note, we'd like to share our appreciation and gratitude individually:

Maria

To my parents, Carol Frazzetta and Joe Giudice, thank you for believing in my artistic sensibilities from a very young age.

To my husband, Scott Allen, thank you for still loving your hardworking wife despite the many nights and weekends that went into creating this book.

To my amazing children, Max and Olivia, thank you for bringing endless joy into my life every single day.

And to Christopher Ireland, my mentor, my co-author, my friend, thank you for an incredible collaborative and co-creative relationship.

Christopher

To my mother, Jeanne Ireland, thank you for giving birth to me first. This turns out to have been crucially important to my becoming a DEO. To my father, Bill Ireland, thank you for giving me the courage to take risks and speak my mind. To my grandmother, Thelma Ireland, a special thank you for showing me that writing can be a career.

To my husband, Davis Masten, thank you for going on vacation without me so I could finish this book. More seriously, thank you for always believing in my dreams and supporting them with all your heart.

To my children, extended family and friends, thank you for letting me ignore you for months without repercussions. At least, none that I know of yet.

And to Maria Giudice, my co-author, my friend, and my inspiration, thank you for saying "yes" when I asked if I could join you in this incredible co-creative journey. What a kick-ass collaborator you are!

Credits:

Project editor: Michael J. Nolan

Research and strategic insight: Radhika Bhalia

Book design: Albertson Design

Information graphic design: Andrew Deming

Copyediting: Gretchen Dykstra, Dykstra Editorial

Book production: David Van Ness

Production coordination: Maureen Forys, Happenstance Type-O-Rama

Translations of DEO interviews:
Julie Prager, 24/7 Transcripts

Proofreading: Patricia Pane

Indexing: Rebecca Plunkett

ABOUT THE AUTHORS

Maria Giudice

Innovator, artist, protagonist, and positive pro-vocateur—Maria Giudice has pursued a vision of intelligent, elegant, people-centered design throughout her professional life. Her grasp of the pragmatic, the authentic, and the essential have kept Maria at the forefront of the intersection of design and business for over 20 years.

Under Maria's leadership, Hot Studio, the experience design firm she founded in 1997, grew into a full-service creative agency with offices in San Francisco and New York City. Along the way, Maria shaped Hot into a people-centered product in its own right—a company that people wanted to work at, and clients loved to work with. Hot Studio was named to *Inc. Magazine*'s Top 5,000 fastest-growing businesses every year since 2008 through 2013, and in 2011 was inducted into the *San Francisco Business Times*' Hall of Fame.

Maria's career began in Richard Saul Wurman's East Coast office, where she was an early practitioner in the then-nascent fields of information architecture and design. Her experience led to work as co-author and designer of several award-winning books, including *Elements of Web Design,* a guide for print designers crossing over to the Web, and *Web Design Essentials.*

Maria has more than 20 years of experience working with and mentoring people from different disciplines. Known for her candor and wit, she has spoken about design and the power of collaboration at conferences throughout the U.S. and abroad, including TEDxPresidio, SXSW, and AIGA's Design Conference. She teaches regularly at the University of Hawaii at Manoa and in California College of the Arts' DMBA and MFA programs.

Maria holds a BFA from Cooper Union. She was recognized as Woman Entrepreneur of the Year by the Women's Initiative, a Bay Area nonprofit that helps provide economic opportunity and education to low-income, high-promise women. In 2012, Maria was named an AIGA Fellow in recognition of her impact in raising the standards of excellence and conduct within the design community.

In 2013 Facebook acquired the talented people of Hot Studio; Maria now works as Director of Product Design at Facebook.

Christopher Ireland

Ethnographer, strategist, idea generator, and alliance builder—Christopher Ireland started her career with the notion that businesses could benefit from a better understanding of people and culture. Her ability to create simple explanations of complex human behavior and to translate those insights into effective design and development strategies attracted clients from both technology and consumer goods companies, including Microsoft, HP, Pepsi, Levis, Gap and more.

As a founder and CEO of Cheskin, a firm that pioneered design research in Silicon Valley, Christopher and her partners had ringside seats to unrivaled feats of creation, innovation, and reinvention. Beginning in the early 1990's, she lead teams exploring notions like how trends move through the teen population, how music relates to mood, the history of residential architectural styles, the power of play, the cultural and behavioral differences between girls and boys, the emerging culture of "cool" in China, the development of trust online, and the meaning of color around the globe—to name just a few. She and her partners sold Cheskin in 2007, and walked away with their sanity mostly intact.

At heart, Christopher is an entrepreneur. During her career at Cheskin, she contributed to hundreds of product launches working with tiny startups and giant monopolies. She continues to satisfy that drive to create new ventures by teaching entrepreneurship at California College of the Arts (CCA) and mentoring startups as the co-founder of Mix & Stir Studio, an incubator for design-driven technology companies.

Christopher has an MBA from the UCLA Anderson School of Management. She has written numerous magazine articles on strategy and design and most recently co-authored the highly rated book *China's New Culture of Cool.*